Foreword by Bestselling Author of *Toughen Up!*

CLAUDE HAMILTON

THICK
SKINNED

Why Caring Too Much about What Other People Think and
Say Is Holding You Back—And What to Do about It

LIFE Leadership Essentials Series

OBSTACLÉS
PRESS

First Edition, November 2014
10 9 8 7 6 5 4 3

Published by:

Obstaclés Press
200 Commonwealth Court
Cary, NC 27511

lifeleadership.com

ISBN: 978-0-9909619-0-1

Scriptures marked "NIV" are taken from the HOLY BIBLE, NEW INTERNATIONAL VERSION®. NIV®. Copyright © 1973, 1978, 1984 by International Bible Society. Used by permission of Zondervan. All rights reserved worldwide.

Cover design and layout by Norm Williams, nwa-inc.com

Printed in the United States of America

Everyone gets knocked down.
Winners get back up.
—ORRIN WOODWARD

The uniform of
leadership is thick skin.
—CHRIS BRADY

CONTENTS

PART III: Four More Powerful Helps

FOREWORD

by Claude Hamilton

One day, I was sitting with a couple who have since become great friends, and they introduced me to their wonderful son and daughters. They told me the amazing story of how they had adopted their son from the country of Haiti when he was very young and why they wanted to adopt him in particular. Elaborating on all the obstacles and struggles they had to overcome to get the little boy to Canada, they shared the immense joy they felt every single day in knowing they had made the right decision to adopt him.

Then the conversation turned to business, and they asked me for perspective on how to deal with one particular family member who seemed to be very against a new business they had started. They were deeply hurt emotionally and couldn't understand why this family member would be such a critic. I told them that anything they were going to do in life that was worthwhile would attract critics. And to illustrate my point, I asked them if every single family member and friend had been super positive and supportive when they announced their decision to adopt a young boy from another country who couldn't even speak the same language! Immediately, I knew they understood. The look on their faces showed they remembered the people who had called them crazy back then and were extremely happy that they hadn't let a few critics change their minds about making that precious boy a part of their family.

As we go through our lives, we will all be criticized, not just for trying to be successful at something but also simply for our everyday decisions: what we decide to study in school, where we go to school, what career path we take, who we date, who we marry, how many kids we have, what we name our children, and on and on and on. But especially when we try to march to the beat of a different drummer and rise above mediocrity, the critics seem to come out of their holes in the ground to "help" us on our way!

I used to think that the best way to deal with criticism was a witty comeback, maybe some profanity, and finally a threat of mild violence as well as internalizing the offence and holding it against the person forever! But I have since learned how wrong that response is. I definitely have never seen it work well! Sadly, what I have seen is far too many people giving up on their endeavors and letting their dreams slip away because they don't know how to handle criticism.

Knowing the right way to handle criticism is crucial. Every successful person I have ever met, read about, or listened to has one thing in common: they have all faced criticism. So it is important for anyone who wants to be successful and accomplish anything worthwhile in life to anticipate criticism, prepare for it, and learn how to deal with it properly. This spectacular book, *Thick-Skinned*, is the perfect way to do that. It is a complete and in-depth discussion on the subject of dealing with critics and will help you understand why they exist and why anyone who attempts anything will attract them. It also reveals the psychology of why criticism hurts so much and why we can sometimes ignore the cheers of thousands and allow the lone voice of one critic to derail us. And most important of all, it teaches many techniques and methods for handling and overcoming criticism so it can never stand in your way of achieving your dreams.

When Orrin Woodward and Chris Brady first approached me about the concept of a leadership development engine, I knew they would produce the highest-caliber information that was principles-based and would truly help people live the lives they've always wanted. This is why I so greatly appreciate the LIFE Leadership Essentials Series. Many books that teach success only lightly cover the multiple areas and topics encompassed in the lifelong, never-ending journey to excellence. But the LIFE Leadership Essentials Series books take each topic and break it down and cover all the angles so thoroughly that you find yourself rereading them again and again and receiving information and insights you previously missed each time. And this addition to the series is no different. The nuggets of wisdom and well-explained concepts make this book not only a great read but essential to your well-being and success.

I heard once that we should never give up the admiration of many for the criticism of a few. I know this book will help you keep criticism in perspective and deal with it the right way. Criticism is actually a blessing when you understand it and can learn to have a positive thick skin! As Chris Brady often says, "The uniform of a leader is thick skin!" So read this book, put on the leader's uniform, and go live the life you've always wanted!

Fight fiercely!

Yours in victory,
Claude Hamilton
Bestselling Author of *Toughen Up!*

INTRODUCTION

Common sense is not so common.
— VOLTAIRE

When asked what he would tell his younger self if he could go back in time and give one piece of advice, former U.S. Secretary of Labor Robert Reich replied: "I'd say, 'If you want to have any impact on the world, you're going to need a very thick skin, and you might as well develop that as early as possible.'"[1]

There are at least three key nuggets of wisdom in this advice. First, everyone should have some desire to impact the world, to do something good, something that matters. None of us should aim for mediocrity. We all have greatness within, if only we choose to apply it.

Many people want to be leaders but find out along the way that success attracts criticism. For a lot of people, this is a real surprise. They tend to think that success will be easier to achieve than it really is, that it will take less work than it actually does, and that everyone who achieves it will be universally loved and admired.

But all real leaders know that success naturally brings competitors, critics, and detractors. Effectively preparing for this early on will help any leader more successfully achieve his or her goals and dreams in life. It is also essential in helping others become leaders — which is something all genuine leaders care about.

Those who aren't prepared for such challenges will frequently find themselves distracted, upset, or unfocused during important times when their leadership is most needed.

> Those who aren't prepared for the challenges that success naturally brings will frequently find themselves distracted, upset, or unfocused during important times when their leadership is most needed.

That's what this book is all about: helping leaders know what to expect and what to do when negative criticism inevitably comes.

Get Thick

Second, if you want to do important things in life, you're going to need a thick skin. This doesn't come naturally for most people. But it can be learned. And if you do learn it, you will save yourself a lot of heartache, frustration, and inner struggle in life.

Try a simple exercise. Go to a grocery store and look at the tabloid magazines on the shelves. Find the most extreme headlines and covers you can, and read them over. By the way, while this is shallow and ridiculous reading for nearly everyone, for leaders and potential leaders, it can serve an important purpose. But just do a little of it, not a lot. Specifically, read the outlandish and other critical headlines and sincerely ask yourself, "How would I feel if it was my name in these headlines?"

Really think about it. How would you feel? The truth is, as all top leaders have learned, it's almost impossible to guess how you'd feel. When the name in a critical article, report, or even online rant by someone nobody has ever heard of is *yours*, it usually hits you right in the gut. At least this is what happens the first time.

> **When the name in a critical article, report, or even online rant by someone nobody has ever heard of is *yours*, it usually hits you right in the gut.**

For some people, the resulting stress lasts for a long time, even years. In fact, some people never quite get over it. This is why developing the right kind of thick skin is so critical. And the earlier you learn what to do and how to do it effectively, the sooner you can move to higher and higher levels of leadership. Also, the better you learn how to have a positive thick skin, the better you'll be as a leader.

As we already mentioned, if you do something really important in life, criticism naturally follows. But it is more than worth it. It is so much better to face detractors than to hunker down, hide your candle under a bushel, and just avoid doing great things. Mediocrity is the worst scenario, and honestly, even mediocre people get their share of negativity and

> **Mediocrity is the worst scenario, and honestly, even mediocre people get their share of negativity and criticism in life.**

criticism in life. Wouldn't you rather be doing something great along the way?

This doesn't mean becoming closed off or unresponsive to feedback, of course. Being *positively* thick-skinned is exactly the opposite. It makes you better at responding to genuine needs for change and improvement because you can quickly and effectively differentiate between helpful feedback and the kind of vitriol that leaders sometimes have to deal with.

Criticism Is a Blessing

The truth is that while criticism is part of any real success, it is actually a very small part. The problem is that it can feel like the main thing in your life, if you aren't prepared. And if you let it, it can literally take over your life. This is why it is essential for leaders and potential leaders to plan ahead and grow a positive thick skin.

For example, when twenty or forty thousand people admire and want to learn from a leader, while one person for some reason dislikes the leader and decides to go on the attack, it makes no sense for the one — rather than the forty thousand — to determine how the leader feels this month. But as many experienced leaders can attest, the negative venom of the one can cause sleepless nights and lots of anxiety unless the leader knows how to respond.

In fact, the bitter bite of one or just a few critics can cause enough distraction in your heart and mind to cause you to do a poor job in serving the forty thousand or the three million. If this lasts a day, it doesn't do much damage. But if it lasts for weeks, months, or years, it can significantly reduce the quality of your leadership.

This makes no *logical* sense, of course, because you should obviously listen to the fifty thousand rather than the one. But that's the problem with a thin skin: it makes you overly sensitive and highly vulnerable to any and all negatives. That's bad. It can, in fact, be devastating if you let it. It may not be *logical*, but it is *actual* because it's *emotional*.

Another problem comes when you as a leader develop a *negative* thick skin. When this occurs, you stop learning from legitimate suggestions, and you can become negative and go angrily on the attack yourself. You become so thick that you don't let anything in. Clearly, this is also detrimental to great leadership.

Seeing It as It Really Is

The goal, the solution, is a truly *positive* thick skin, one that allows you to stay focused on what really matters, to see that forty thousand positives versus one negative is a fantastic ratio, as is anything where you have more positives than negatives. In politics for example, there is a name for people who are loved by 50.1 percent of the nation and widely and even vocally disliked by 49.9 percent; the name is "Madame President" or "Mr. Prime Minister."

> **The goal, the solution, is a truly *positive* thick skin, one that allows you to stay focused on what really matters.**

Again, being positively thick-skinned means putting things in true perspective, not getting emotionally swept away by the words of naysayers or critics or by personal attacks. Reading a few tabloid headlines with this in mind makes it clear that anyone with success needs to relax and accept that a bit of criticism is just part of doing anything at high levels of success.

We're not suggesting that you make a habit of reading the tabloids, since they are, as you know, mostly junk and a colossal waste of time for most people. But they can be helpful to leaders in two main ways. When you want to start developing a thick skin in order to prepare for more leadership, a trip to the store to peruse a few of the head-lines and insert your name in them will help you get a sense of how ridiculous most unconstructive criticism really is.

This is an important place to start. It can help inoculate you against unfair attacks when they come someday.

Later, when a time comes as a leader that someone really attacks you unfairly, criticizing you in surprising and extreme ways, you can repeat this process. After reading what the tabloids say about celebrities, you'll realize that (A) the whole criticism genre is pretty ridiculous; (B) the things people say are almost always false or at least falsely skewed; (C) the media frequently lies because its focus is sometimes sales and ratings rather than truth; (D) other people are getting criticized a whole lot worse than you are; (E) the more successful you are, the more criticism you receive; and (F) the truly successful people getting criticized just ignore the drivel and move on with better and better successes. That's the ultimate response.

Again, for most people, reading a tabloid is a terrible waste of time. But for a leader, reading the front cover of three tabloids once in your life can be very helpful — if you do it the right way. Just read the cover of three tabloids one time, and see how ridiculous the media can be. Then don't read tabloids again — ever. But remember the lesson: critics deserve little or no credence!

This lesson is vital for top leaders.

Start Now

Third, the earlier you learn to be positively thick-skinned, the better. You probably already realize that you care too much about what people think or say about you. Most people do. But this "caring too much" holds many people

> **The earlier you learn to be positively thick-skinned, the better.**

back in pursuing and accomplishing their goals. Success comes to top leaders because somewhere along the way they decided to:

1. Keep doing the right things (and great things) regardless of what other people think, say, or do
2. Stay in the game and pursue their life purpose no matter what

To repeat this vitally important point, consider what business leaders and bestselling authors Chris Brady and Orrin Woodward wrote in their book *LIFE*:

Life for Orrin is much easier since he decided two things: 1) to press on regardless of the actions of others, and 2) that he was in the game no matter what. This released the stress and anxiety felt by most people when not truly committed to a course of action.

Leaders make a decision, back that decision with full commitment, and make the decision right with overwhelming passion and effort....

Success in life is simply a matter of staying focused on the areas that you control while surrendering to God the areas that are outside of your control.[2]

> "Success in life is simply a matter of staying focused on the areas that you control while surrendering to God the areas that are outside of your control."
> — Chris Brady and Orrin Woodward

This is the core of becoming positively thick-skinned. Do the right things and pursue your life mission regardless of how anyone else treats you, including detractors or enemies. Moreover, remember that criticism nearly always comes from a very small number of people compared to those who appreciate your leadership.

When you take the right action in response to negativity, your response sets an
example of courage and
wisdom for others, making you
an even better leader. It also
teaches you how to disagree
with others—including criticizing ideas or programs
instead of attacking people—
and the importance of getting

> **Remember that criticism nearly always comes from a very small number of people compared to those who appreciate your leadership.**

the facts right *before* you reach conclusions. These are vital
leadership lessons, and nothing teaches them more effectively than facing your own opposition.

Finally, embrace the fact that your success is going to
include some detractors and that this actually can help
you be a better and more successful leader—if you know
how to prepare and respond in the right ways, if you know
the steps of being positively thick-skinned. This book is all
about learning the best ways to prepare and respond.

Almost everybody wants to be admired and loved, but
almost nobody wants to be crit-
icized—except for top leaders,
who have learned that all of
these things are a signal that
they're doing something right.
They really are.

> **If nobody disagrees with you, your leadership likely isn't accomplishing much.**

If nobody disagrees with you,
your leadership likely isn't accomplishing much. Having
a few naysayers is a test of your direction and success.

And when you know how to be positively thick-skinned, all valid criticism will help you make good changes, and any other attacks will add strength to your successes.

So let's learn how to be thick-skinned — and, even more important, *positively* thick-skinned. This will be a huge benefit to your leadership for the rest of your life.

PART I

WHY YOU ARE THIN-SKINNED

Necessity compels me…
—DANTE

1

THE LEADERSHIP SURPRISE

THE SHOCK OF SUCCESS

Are you good men and true?

—SHAKESPEARE

Anyone who has achieved any real success has been there. You dreamed and fantasized about doing something great, about accomplishing amazing things, and about achieving the miraculous. In all your daydreams and visualizations of the future, you faced tough odds, worked hard and reached for inner greatness to overcome them, and then smiled and felt deeply satisfied as thousands of people—maybe millions—applauded and cheered your hard-won success.

But when you get there, after surmounting all the roadblocks and challenges of succeeding, you receive the shock of your life: In addition to the many people cheering for your victory, there are also a few vocal, committed, and even heated critics who seem enraged that you didn't fail. This isn't what you expected!

You thought everyone would love you. After all, what you accomplished is amazing — hard, challenging, and rare. Anyone and everyone should be impressed, you tell yourself. But a few people apparently didn't get the memo. They seem to think you must have manipulated or cheated to get where you are. They think your achievement is just luck and that you are somehow a bad person. And they're committed to telling everyone how bad you are, even if they have to make things up to get their message across.

> **In addition to the many people cheering for your victory, there are also a few vocal, committed, and even heated critics who seem enraged that you didn't fail.**

Haters Beware

In the Internet age, such people are known by the delightful title of "haters" or "trolls." They slink around online and seem to hate everything. They find a way to criticize and tear down even the most dedicated and successful people in every walk of life — politics, sports, business, medicine, family, leadership, and so forth.

Read almost any forum online, and a hater or two eventually joins the discussion. Hang around the water cooler in almost any business, and eventually a hater will start sharing his or her views. Attend any seminar or even go on vacation, and you'll run into a hater who dislikes the hotel, the airline, the speaker, the food, the clothes you are wearing — or even the clothes he or she is wearing!

In fact, when you see it from this angle, it is actually pretty funny. So laugh a little. Some people just plain like to complain. Some like to criticize and attack. In fact, some people spend so much time being haters that they are actually known as online "trolls," people who have made it their goal in life to attack, snipe, criticize, and tear people down. How sad.

Somehow haters seem to think that spending their precious time and life attacking others is a benefit to their own life. Why? Does this actually make them happy? Not at all. Does it make them more successful themselves to tear others down? Just the opposite.

So why do they do it? Do they think attacking others will improve their lives? Did they eat cereal with sour milk this morning? Are they going through a terrible divorce or layoff? After all, as Orrin Woodward teaches, *hurting* people usually seek to hurt people.

Were haters and critics born negative? Is it just easier to criticize than to be successful in life? Or is there some other reason? Very often, vocal critics themselves actually have something to hide. You certainly don't want to waste your life and leadership skills on this path.

The truth is people are people. We all have the ability to choose greatness, mediocrity, or destructive thoughts and behaviors. Any one of us could choose to become a hater. But top leaders would rather put their energy and effort into an important life purpose and mission. They'd rather be a success and help other people succeed as well.

> **Top leaders would rather put their energy and effort into an important life purpose and mission.**

Again, the fact that a few people choose to be haters is a little funny—like the reality that in every family reunion there are two or three people who just make you shake your head. You have to laugh, just to make sense of things.

So laugh. There are going to be a few haters and even trolls in life. It's okay. Just don't let yourself be one of them. And don't let their negativity influence your hard work to do good. You have too much success ahead. You have too many great things to do. Let the haters be haters. Laugh at their theatrics, and get on with your important life purpose.

Don't be surprised when a few people are haters. Just realize this is a signal that you've arrived, that you're doing something that matters and attracts attention. That's good! Now focus on doing more of it, doing it better, and having an even greater impact.

Good News

The truth is that having haters is actually very good news. *New York Times* bestselling author Chris Brady noticed an important pattern when studying book reviews on Amazon. Many books with a lot of five-star ratings also have a few one-star reviews, while books without any bad reviews often don't have a bunch of five-star raving reviews. The majority of books with no bad ratings receive mostly mediocre ratings or no ratings at all—people just don't care enough to bother with a review. But, again, those with lots of high praise pretty much always have a few low ratings. If it's good enough to be loved, it's going to rub a few people wrong. If nobody dislikes it, hardly anyone truly loves it either.

> If it's good enough to be loved, it's going to rub a few people wrong. If nobody dislikes it, hardly anyone truly loves it either.

This pattern is repeated in many ways. Bestselling author Claude Hamilton wrote the following in his book *Toughen Up!*:

Paul Newman once noted, "A man with no enemies is a man with no character." This is a particularly important reality because we should judge people not only by their friends but also by what they stand for and what (and whom) they stand against.

For example, a friend of mine told me the story of how he started a small philanthropy and spent a great deal of his time fund-raising to keep it going and growing. He traveled to Edmonton, Alberta, to meet with a particularly wealthy potential donor who had expressed interest in supporting his organization and its cause.

After several hours of discussing the organization and its leadership, finances, and plans for expansion, the donor turned to my friend and said, "I'm very impressed with what you are doing. I just have one more question for you. In what ways have you and your organization been attacked and opposed?"

My friend was happy to report that they had received only support, no real opposition of any kind.

The donor looked at him thoughtfully and then replied, "That's too bad. Well, if your charity really amounts to something, you'll get your share of opposition. When that happens, come back, and I'll be happy to donate to help your cause."

With that, the donor ended the meeting, and my friend flew home. Needless to say, he was surprised by the turn of events. But more experienced leaders understand what the wealthy donor was saying because the character — of people and institutions — is truly revealed and defined only in times of serious adversity. And even more to the point, our character has not really been tested until it meets strong opposition.[1]

When criticism or opposition comes, it's time for a big smile! It's time to take a deep breath, relax, and realize that you're on track for big things. This is the right response, and it's the natural response if you have a positive thick skin.

If, on the other hand, you are thin-skinned, you'll likely respond with anxiety, worry, and distraction from your current projects that really matter. You might even get angry and go on the attack yourself, trying to bring down the hater who said negative things about you. All these responses hurt you and your mission.

There is, of course, a time for a wise response. But often the best response is to just keep succeeding. When a response actually is needed, it should be brief and to the point, clarify the facts in nonemotional and nondefensive language, and not add to the drama. You've got more important things to do. You're a leader now, after all. How do we know? Because you're doing enough that people who don't even know you personally are criticizing you. Congratulations! You have haters. You're doing at least something right. Keep doing what you're doing! More success is just ahead.

> **If you haven't been misquoted, you probably haven't said anything that matters.**

But don't be thin-skinned and let yourself get distracted. As Claude Hamilton said:

Enjoy the struggle. People only become great when they have to struggle, adapt, and overcome. So if you face difficulty in living your dreams and achieving your life purpose, congratulations! You're probably on the right track. At the very least, you're doing something right.

As the old saying goes, "If you haven't been misquoted, you probably haven't said anything that matters. And if you haven't been attacked, you probably aren't doing much that will really make a difference."[2]

Or as journalist Barbara Walters put it, "If everybody likes you, you're doing something wrong."

When haters show up, it's an indication that you're starting to be a leader. So get positive and keep going! Things are going to get exciting now.

2

THE UNIVERSAL SEARCH FOR ADMIRATION

WHY YOU CARE SO MUCH WHAT PEOPLE THINK AND SAY ABOUT YOU

You [humans] are fond of spectacles.

—TERTULLIAN

We all have a limbic brain (some people call it the "reptile brain" or the "monkey brain") that operates mostly on the basis of instinct. It senses something and reacts immediately. It is the "fight or flight" brain that tells us that a bear just walked into our path and we have just enough time to run to the nearest tree—or not enough time to get away so we'd better pull out our knife or play dead.

The limbic brain focuses on survival, so it doesn't take its time brainstorming options or analyzing the best reactions in any situation. It just acts.

> **The limbic brain focuses on survival, so it doesn't take its time brainstorming options or analyzing the best reactions in any situation. It just acts.**

Of course, the thinking aspect of our brain has the ability to take over when needed, to identify that we can override the limbic brain and make better choices, to really think things through, but the first reaction is usually rooted in the instinctive brain. The limbic brain's first question upon meeting a new person is whether this is a possible friend or a potential enemy. Its first thought in any new situation is to question whether this is a chance for benefit or a possible danger.

Not surprisingly, the limbic part of our brain is more powerful when the person or situation is potentially dangerous. We are naturally almost hardwired to let the limbic brain take over the thinking brain when a lion walks into our path or a gunman threatens us in a dark parking lot.

Likewise, the limbic brain kicks in when our kids are in danger or our livelihood is threatened. Hearing "Mr. Jones, the IRS is on line three" or "Your son's school called. He's been in a fight, and they need you in the principal's office right away" creates an immediate limbic response for most people.

Overrides

If these types of situations and calls happen routinely, your thinking brain will learn to compensate and override the intense limbic response, but if it's the first time for any such event, your limbic chemicals can create powerful reactions. Your breathing rate immediately increases, your heart rate jumps, and your hearing and seeing of routine things around you fades out of conscious notice. This is a long-studied and well-documented response.

In dealing with the lion or the gunman, this may be exactly what your body needs to survive, but when twenty thousand people are cheering and one hater tells lies about you, the limbic response causes real problems. Put bluntly, the limbic chemicals are stronger and more intense than the normal brain functions, so in fact, your physical response to the one naysayer is a lot more severe than the endorphin rush you experience when the thousands are cheering. This is called "being thin-skinned."

You can train your brain to see this differently, and as a result, it will respond differently. But without such training, your limbic response will usually take over, and you'll routinely make bad decisions when you feel even a little threatened.

Again, your limbic system is designed to put threats at the forefront of your consciousness

> Your limbic system is designed to put threats at the forefront of your consciousness so you'll forget everything else and take immediate and extreme action to survive.

so you'll forget everything else and take immediate and extreme action to survive. Adrenaline pumps through your body, and you gear up to run fast or smash things.

When you respond in this manner to something that really isn't a threat—because your limbic brain is yelling at you to run or fight or scream or strike—you generally make very bad choices. Top leaders learn to control such impulses, and in fact, learning to do this is a vital part of becoming a good leader.

Lions and Tigers and Haters, Oh My!

The fact is that the limbic brain is addicted to caring too much what other people think and say about you. Its whole purpose is to sense any threat as quickly as possible, allowing you time to get away from the lion or bear, and blow that threat far out of proportion—since waiting around to see if the lion is actually going to charge you is highly unsafe. Better to run now and then observe the lion's intentions from a tall tree than to stop and analyze the real threat. Or, at least, so says the limbic brain.

As you can see, the limbic brain puts a premium on immediate responses and on quickly running from or attacking any potential threat—before it can do you harm. As we said, this may be the perfect response to a lion, but it is usually totally wrong when a hater or detractor, or even someone who has always been your friend, says something mean about you.

The John Adams Rule

American founding father John Adams taught that almost everyone wants to be admired, recognized, and congratulated.

They want honors, public attention, awards, promotions, and glory. Many schools, families, businesses, military units, social groups, and even nations use badges, gold stars, grades, promotions, rewards, awards, and so on to help people do the right thing. In fact, such offers can create powerful positive incentives for success.

Even more important, Adams said, most people deeply fear criticism, ridicule, pity, or verbal attack. Since these emotions are so strong, it is amazing what many people will do to elicit praise or to avoid disapproval.

We almost all want to be liked — by everyone, if possible, all the time. But while this completely human tendency can at times encourage us to do good things, it more often holds us back. Many people live in fear of taking any risks or stepping out in anything they do, frequently choosing mediocrity over greatness in order to avoid any chance of criticism. But as championship coach Bill Walsh put it: "Before you can win the fight, you've got to be *in* the fight."[1]

> "Before you can win the fight, you've got to be *in* the fight."
> — Bill Walsh

The John Adams Rule is that all great success in life comes from mastering this tendency and *choosing* your response rather than just instinctively reacting. Stephen Covey made this the first of his *7 Habits*, and the great

Viktor Frankl called it the space between stimulus and response. Since we all want admiration, and nobody wants to be criticized, we can only master ourselves by becoming impervious to what other people think or say about us.

Specifically, Adams taught, we must take our own counsel—or at least only wise counsel. We must expect that people will say nice things about us and not allow their flattery to influence our choices. We must also realize that some people will say negative, hurtful, or even untrue things about us and not allow their words to influence our feelings, decisions, or actions.

This is easier said than done, but in this book, we'll learn how to effectively master this essential leadership skill. The solution is to train our limbic brains and our thinking brains to recategorize what really is a threat and what is actually an exciting opportunity.

Everyone knows the old proverb about turning lemons into lemonade, but the difference between top leaders and others is that true leaders actually turn this advice into a habit. They make it a skill. They learn to master their limbic and thinking brains.

They train themselves to turn negatives into opportunities and to turn their brain responses to critics or even haters from limbic fear generators to opportunity monitors. Instead of fight or flight, their brains go directly to creativity, initiative, and innovation.

In short, instead of sensing a danger when they are faced with negatives, they experience a positive emotional boost of competitive excitement. They do more of what's already working and do it better!

Mastering this ability is powerful, and it turns regular people into leaders and good leaders into great ones. In the pages ahead, we're going to learn how to master this skill.

3

THE FOUR ALLEGIANCES

WHOM DO YOU WANT TO IMPRESS?

Everybody's friend is nobody's.
— ARTHUR SCHOPENHAUER

Everyone wants to impress someone, and the person to whom you choose to give your highest allegiance will in large part determine your level of success, achievement, and contribution in life. Each of the four top allegiances, as outlined by *New York Times* bestselling author Oliver DeMille, has pros and cons, but most people choose the wrong allegiances. As a result, they build their lives around impressing the wrong people.

This is the source of the 80/20 Rule, sometimes called the 90/10 or 95%/5% Rule. The

> "Leaders do what ought to be done whether their deeds are known by thousands or known by no one."
> —Orrin Woodward

5 percent choose the right allegiances, and this makes all the difference. *New York Times* bestselling author Orrin Woodward says, "Leaders do what ought to be done whether their deeds are known by thousands or known by no one."[1]

The four major allegiances are God, Bad, Other People, and some Certain Person or Group. In other words, everyone tends to want to impress someone, and we nearly all choose one of these four to try to impress.

Tom's Story

Let's think about this more deeply by following the leadership choices of a young man named Tom. Tom is known to his friends as a positive person who loves life. In high school and college, he enjoyed social events, playing tennis, and riding motorcycles, and he was a pretty good student—eventually studying communications and thinking about a career in journalism.

During his sophomore year in college, he took a sales job in order to pay the bills and found that he was good at it. He liked people, and he genuinely cared about their needs. This translated into excellent service, and Tom's sales soared.

During the next summer break, Tom started a new business working with a couple of his friends, and he realized that growing his own business would be a great opportunity. He deferred his enrollment in college in order to really establish his business. Within eighteen months, he was making good money, and the business clearly had a bright future.

As Tom worked every day on his budding business, he became increasingly excited. He was helping a lot of people and seeing more and more success. Even the challenges and down times became opportunities to push himself, learn, and improve. In his mind's eye, he saw a future of real leadership. In fact, this became more of a reality every month.

The Arrival of a Choice

At this point, if not before, Tom faced a vitally important choice: To whom would he give his allegiance? Tom, like most people, hadn't given this decision much thought. He had just "gone with the flow" and unconsciously adopted a desire to be liked and admired by people, to fit in, and to be accepted and popular.

The Certain Person or Group Tom wanted to like him (a father, an uncle, a past coach, a community mentor, a mother-in-law, or possibly the popular crowd he hung out with or the members of his former high school tennis team) was determined by his life experiences. Whatever the Certain Person or Group, they had, without their knowledge, become his allegiance.

He wanted them to like him, and he wanted to impress them, so he made choices he thought they would approve and admire. He instinctively avoided decisions he thought they would dislike or question.

This is the power of an allegiance. It significantly influences a person's deepest thoughts, ideas, feelings, and choices. In direct, though often subtle or even invisible, ways it encourages or discourages certain decisions and actions.

This can be a very good thing for Tom, or it can be a serious problem. It can inspire greatness and motivate him to do hard things that matter. By contrast, it can block progress by discouraging any risk-taking and emphasizing mediocrity.

If Tom's main subconscious goals center around impressing a Certain Person or Group, this will almost always hold him back from achieving his potential because when hard leadership choices arise, he won't know his own mind or heart. He'll want to know what his Certain Group or Person thinks, and he'll frequently find himself afraid or tenuous when he most needs to be strong and committed.

Oh, Fickle Man!

The fundamental problem with allegiances to a Certain Person or Group, or to Other People in general, is that these people constantly change their minds. For example, Tom's allegiance may be to a father-in-law he wants to impress or to his popular-crowd friends from high school. But if he decides to get off the normal career-training path of college and instead start a business, these allegiances are likely to have shifting views of his choice.

At first, when he takes the risk of entrepreneurial creativity, they're sure to warn him about all the pitfalls of risk and the danger of trying to become a leader. They'll tell him a dozen or more stories of people they know who tried to start businesses and failed.

> **The fundamental problem with allegiances to a Certain Person or Group, or to Other People in general, is that these people constantly change their minds.**

They'll purse their lips, shake their heads slowly, wrinkle their brows, and repeat every doubt and fear they've ever had about trying to do something big. If Tom's Certain Person or Group is a parent or a romantic interest, such body language can be especially hard to overlook. They will sound supportive and claim to be objective, stressing that they just can't imagine a way for this to turn out well for him.

If Tom holds strongly to his goals and moves ahead despite this initial opposition, they'll ask him about it every chance they get—and in the interim, they'll notice every failed risk taker and every statistic about how difficult his path can be. They'll forward him every negative opinion they can find online.

Each time they talk to him, they'll be further prepared to point out the "flaws" of his actions. And they'll do this without reciprocity—meaning that if Tom brings up any concerns about *their* path, whatever it is, they'll be offended that he has the audacity to give them unsolicited advice (even though this is precisely what they are giving him).

Note that most of this will be truly, genuinely well-intentioned. Such people really do mean to help him, not tear him down. And note also that this kind of dream-killing conversation will happen no matter who is the object of Tom's allegiance.

But when these people are Tom's Certain Person or Group and one of his main goals in life is to impress them, he's a lot more likely to listen to them and give up on his dreams. This happens frequently.

In fact, if Tom's allegiance is to Other People in general, meaning that he really wants to be admired by all and criticized by none, he will be especially weak at dealing with any negative opinions about his chosen path. This applies to *all* career paths and life choices, not just entrepreneurship, since there are always a few people who disagree with anything.

If we didn't have such disagreements, we wouldn't have, for example, any great literature, since such differing opinions about every life choice are the whole point of *Pride and Prejudice, Sense and Sensibility, Jane Eyre, War and Peace, Les Misérables, Don Quixote*, and every play by Shakespeare, among others. This is also the main subject of almost every popular television

> **If we didn't have disagreements about life choices, we wouldn't have any great literature!**

show — whether action, drama, sitcom, reality show, or soap opera. It is even, in reality, the truth behind every good book on world history and also the nightly news.

If Tom somehow keeps going anyway (though he likely won't if his allegiance to Other People or a Certain Person or Group is too strong) and begins to have some real success, many people will suddenly switch their views. This is where their fickle nature kicks in.

They'll introduce Tom to friends by noting his amazing achievements, and they'll suddenly be very excited by his progress. They'll assure him: "I knew you might be one of the few who could actually do this!"

When Tom runs into the natural struggles of continuing his early successes, they'll usually switch their stance right back: "I always worried that it wouldn't last, Tom. It's just too difficult to be a leader. Great leaders are few and far between. When are you going to get back on the normal path? There's still time, you know."

Then, again, when Tom keeps working hard and pushes past the period of struggles needed in any kind of real success and begins to really build big, they'll act as if they always knew he would do it. They'll maintain this view long term, except that each time he runs into any major problems, they'll revert to head shaking, furrowed brows, and discussions about how they knew this would probably fail.

It's not that people are all bad or purposely fickle; it's just that they naturally react to whatever seems most realistic at the moment. When something changes, they react to that, without thinking it through from the big picture. This is how nearly all people, the 95 percent, so to speak, usually approach life.

A Better Way

If Tom wants to become a real leader, one of the 5 percent, he'll have to learn to see things the way successful leaders view them. But this is almost impossible if his true allegiance is to Other People in general or to a Certain Person or Group in his life.

Great leadership and success are challenging enough without having to constantly feel you are letting down the people you truly want to impress. In fact, if Tom's real, long-term allegiance is to Other People, he will eventually give in to whatever he thinks they will admire and appreciate.

This is why most real leaders, those who successfully choose and continue on the path of great leadership, learn that allegiance to another Person or Group of people doesn't work. They learn to choose God as their allegiance because God isn't fickle or wishy-washy.

> Real leaders, those who successfully choose and continue on the path of great leadership, learn that allegiance to another Person or Group of people doesn't work.

God sees the big picture, and seeking to do His will is the only authentic and solid road to genuine success and leadership. Every other path will eventually let us down.

Those who choose God as their allegiance will always have one standard: to do the right thing. This will hold true, unchangeable, through all the challenges, struggles, and successes of leadership and progress.

Every great leader must learn to do the right thing no matter what people think, and so eventually this is the only allegiance that helps a person become a genuinely great leader. Every other allegiance falls short.

The Worst Allegiance

When introduced to this truth, some will inevitably say: "But I know of some leaders who are actually selfish and bad, who choose terrible things but still seem to gain real wealth, influence, and power — like Stalin or Caligula. Why did they get power?"

The answer is that there is a fourth allegiance that is a commitment to Bad. Some people choose to be impressed only by power and wealth, by position and control over others. This allegiance can be a powerful motivator because it is extremely selfish and self-centered. But, like the mediocre allegiances of impressing Other People in general or always seeking the admiration of a Certain Person or Group, an allegiance to Bad, selfish things always eventually lets us down.

It may lead to some apparent success for a time, but it never brings lasting happiness or genuine peace. It always fails eventually.

If Tom chooses to put his own wants and desires above everything else, to sacrifice his morals, principles, integrity, values, and relationships to seek his egotistical appetites for power, fame, or greed, he'll end up hurting himself and alienating those closest to him. And know this: No matter how glitzy his outward appearances of success, he will be dying inside. This is not the path to success or happiness.

Likewise, with this approach, Tom will never actually learn to grow a positive thick skin. He'll be too selfish, too insecure, and he'll turn angrily on anyone he perceives as a potential threat. He'll tend to blow any small criticism way out of proportion, thinking every word of disagreement is a full-blown coup, a massive attack on his "success."

Many so-called leaders have gained some selfish wealth and power but were also ruined in just this way. It's the Richard Nixon or Chairman Mao approach to life.

You Go, Boy!

If Tom wants to become a real leader, he'll need to choose the right allegiance, a deep commitment to God. This will give him the strength to do the right thing, regardless of what other people think and even when it may look like the less profitable or more difficult choice.

This will teach him to have confidence in the face of any and all criticism and to do the right thing no matter what. Over time, this will help him develop a strong sense of inner security, which is the true positive thick skin.

He'll learn to be open to suggestions, recommendations, constructive feedback, and even criticism that will help him improve. At the same time, he will develop a powerful sense of solid security in who he is and what he stands for, and he'll be truly comfortable in his own skin.

Indeed, he'll have a positive thick skin that allows him to learn from his mistakes and stay strong and focused on doing the right thing and building his life purpose, regardless of what other people think, say, or do.

> **The foundation of a positive thick skin is a dedicated commitment to the right allegiance.**

This is what it means to be positively thick-skinned, and every trustworthy and faithful leader must turn this into a consistent habit and strength. Indeed, the foundation of a positive thick skin is a dedicated commitment to the right allegiance.

Tom's Future

Clearly, there is a huge difference between the future Tom will have if he chooses any of the other three allegiances rather than an allegiance to God. This one choice, and his discipline in following it, will be the most powerful factor that determines the level of his success and the impact of his life's work.

If he chooses poorly, he will never really achieve his potential. If he chooses wisely and maintains this decision through his life, almost nothing can stop him from living his life purpose and doing truly great things. And in all of this, such a choice will make him much more secure, strong, and effective as a person and as a leader.

A Look in the Mirror

In short, many people are thin-skinned for a simple reason: they have the wrong allegiance. They're trying to impress people, so of course they have a thin skin. Most people have never consciously chosen their allegiance, but leadership eventually requires each of us to make this choice on purpose and to choose correctly.

> In short, many people are thin-skinned for a simple reason: they have the wrong allegiance.

People with an allegiance to impressing a Certain Person or Group or Other People in general are nearly always thin-skinned and likely to be swayed by opinions, criticism, and every little problem that comes along. Those whose allegiance is to their own Bad, selfish desires for power, control, fame, greed, or any other unprincipled appetite will burn relationships, hurt those around them, and daily sow the seeds of their own inevitable failure. They will also have the thinnest skin of all because they are consumed with fear of the failure they sense they deserve and know will eventually come.

Those who choose an allegiance to God and do their best to follow true principles and do the right thing on every occasion will have the security of their convictions that allows them to be solid, honorable, trustworthy, and deeply secure. This is the path to a powerfully positive thick skin.

If you find yourself too often thin-skinned, these are the first two questions to answer: Have you firmly chosen the right allegiance, and are you doing enough to consistently live up to it? For as it says in John 15:16 (NIV), "You did not choose me, but I chose you and appointed you so that you might go and bear fruit—fruit that will last."

PART II

HOW TO BECOME POSITIVELY THICK-SKINNED

*It is not titles that reflect honor on men,
but men on their titles.*

—MACHIAVELLI

4

THE DRUCKER PRINCIPLE

THE POWER OF EMULATION

As long as rivers shall run down to the sea,
or shadows touch the mountain slopes,
or stars graze in the vault of heaven,
so long shall your honor, your name, your praises endure.
—Virgil

The great business writer Peter Drucker taught that it is essential for those seeking real success to do one simple thing: follow the advice and example of the right people—not those who claim to be experts, but those who have actually achieved the kind of success you want. This is the power of emulation, and it is incredibly effective.

Say, for example, that you want to learn how to handle your money well. Whom do you go to for advice? Broke people? If you want to get in shape, do you follow the guidance of people who are flabby couch potatoes? When you want a great education, do you take counsel from people who dislike books and would rather just watch TV? Clearly the answer to these questions is a resounding "No!"

> **Follow the advice and example of the right people — not those who claim to be experts, but those who have actually achieved the kind of success you want.**

If you want advice on money, go to people who have it and know how to handle it, such as Chris Brady, Orrin Woodward, and the other founders of LIFE Leadership who collaborated to produce the *Financial Fitness* book. If getting in physical shape is your goal, go to someone who knows how to do it and has demonstrated years of success, such as fitness leader Mark MacDonald. Read his books.

If you want to get an excellent education in the classics, read *A Thomas Jefferson Education*[1] by Oliver DeMille, and if you want to get the most out of your next travel vacation, read *A Month of Italy*[2] by Chris Brady. In short, when you need help improving at something, go to people who have actually done what you want to do and achieved the kind of results you want to have.

> **To learn how to get a thick skin, emulate leaders who have been there and done that.**

This may seem overly obvious, but it's amazing how many people skip this basic truth. To learn how to get a thick skin, emulate leaders who have been there and done that. This is true in every field of success. Emulate those who have what you want.

False Path #1: Groupies

There are several important things to remember and avoid when you emulate people who have been successful in something. First, don't become a zealot. For example, in the music industry, there are people known as "groupies." These zealous fans love to attend the performances of their favorite singers or groups, wait in long lines through the night on the opening day of every new release, keep up to date on every piece of gossip about their favorite artists, and generally dedicate (waste!) a lot of their time doing meaningless things to stay abreast of every article, report, rumor, and word about "their group."

This is what makes them groupies. They spend hours poring over the latest pictures of their number-one star.

The sad reality, even the irony, of the situation is that their favorite artists would never waste their time doing these things. They're too busy writing a new song, practicing for an upcoming performance, living life with loved ones and friends, enjoying free time, working hard to produce the next product, and so on.

In fact, most successful artists would flatly reject the offer to spend their time doing what their groupies do. They would see it as a monumental waste. They'd be totally bored. They'd hate it.

So emulation isn't the same thing as being a groupie. If you want to emulate successful people, study their speeches, writings, interviews, and ideas. Wherever possible, focus on their actual words, not just what someone else has written about them.

If you are emulating a great person from history, like George Washington on leadership or Patrick Henry on boldness, you can find biographies and also collections of their written works and letters. While biographies can be very helpful, their collected writings are even better. Study what they themselves actually wrote and thought and how they responded to challenges and opportunities.

Take lots of notes, write in the margins, highlight and underline, and even memorize particularly moving quotes from those you are learning to emulate. Also, pay special attention to times in their lives when they faced major challenges or very difficult decisions. How did they deal with problems? What choices did they have to make, and why did they make the ones they did? Did they ever make any wrong choices? If so, what did they learn from their mistakes? How did they work with others in challenging situations and circumstances?

Overall, what can you learn from their choices and actions—both good and bad? How can you do better? In what ways can you seriously improve yourself? These kinds of lessons are the key to learning how to emulate.

If the person you seek to emulate is still alive, be careful to respect his or her privacy. You can learn all you need to from his or her public words and actions. In fact, most leaders deal with a lot of people who want to invade their personal time but actually don't follow their public advice very well at all.

Do the opposite. Leave them alone personally (except when direct contact is invited), but work very hard to listen to their speeches and interviews, read their words, and apply them. This is real emulation, and it really works.

> **Most leaders deal with a lot of people who want to invade their personal time but actually don't follow their public advice very well at all.**

Again, don't be a groupie; that's not emulation at all. Be the kind of person the leader you want to emulate would admire and want to spend time with and learn from. That's when you know you are on target.

False Path #2: Posers

In addition to the annoyance of groupies, most successful people have also had to deal with "clones." Clones are people who literally try to copy the leader's work.

As every leader who has had to put up with such frustration knows, emulation doesn't mean copying a person. You don't want to actually be that person. You want to learn from his or her experiences and apply the lessons he or she has gained from both mistakes and triumphs. As *New York Times* bestselling author Austin Kleon put it, "You don't want to *look* like your heroes; you want to *see* like your heroes (emphasis added)."[3]

For example, following the music industry again, there are people who really like a certain artist or band, so they start publicly performing their favorite artist's songs. They sometimes go as far as to put out shadow albums on which they sing all the same songs but try to do them even better. This is usually illegal, and it is almost always in poor taste. The original artist would never do this, so this isn't emulation at all.

In the world of skateboarding, clones are known simply as "posers." It's not a good title either. Posers aren't the real thing; they're just posing as the real thing. That's not emulation. You want to become the real thing—an original, just like the leader you admire.

Learn from those whose success you would like to emulate, but do your own work and earn your own rewards. Don't try to steal from others or capitalize on copying them.

> **Learn from those whose success you would like to emulate, but do your own work and earn your own rewards.**

This kind of personality plagiarism is wrong. Give full credit when you borrow or quote from someone else, and always do your own work. Make them proud that you want to emulate them, not "weirded out" at the way you try to counterfeit their work.

Again, the key is to learn from their example—doing the positive things suggested in the above section on not being a groupie. Read their writings and speeches, and study and follow their recommendations. This is true emulation, and nothing else comes close.

Plus, in all this, add your own creativity. Do your own hard work. As you learn from the success of others and then do your best to apply the lessons they recommend, you'll obtain the best results.

False Path #3: Ignorers

There is a third way *not* to emulate, and this is to simply ignore the successful principles shown by those who have the kind of success you seek. If you are in sales, for example, and you ignore everything that has been proven to work in your field and type of selling, you probably won't sell much.

If you decide to get in shape and hit upon what you like to call the "hundred pieces of sugary cake and twenty bottles of soda pop every week" diet, you probably won't lose weight—or help anyone else get rid of their extra pounds either. In fact, you'll probably cause the opposite result.

Where groupies neglect hard work and just try to feel happy based on the choices and lives of others, posers try to lazily copy the actual work of those they seek to emulate, and ignorers do the opposite. They don't apply any principles of success or listen to those who have proven how to succeed. As a result, they fail. Often. Repeatedly, in fact.

The key to effective emulation is to reject all three of these weak paths. When you want to succeed in any arena, find the people who have been truly successful there, and learn from them. Find out what they did that worked, and emulate it. Find out what principles they valued and applied, and do the same. This leads to successful emulation.

To Be a Success, Watch a Success (and Take Notes!)

To get specific on how to emulate successfully, Peter Drucker suggested turning this process into a bit of science. To become an effective executive, he taught, watch what effective executives do — and don't do — and take notes. Listen to what they say — and don't say — and follow suit.

Pay attention to how they interact with others; the words they use; the way they dress, decorate their offices, and greet people; the way they deal with difficulties or problems; and so on. And always take notes.

> To become an effective executive, watch what effective executives do — and don't do — and take notes.

This applies in many areas of life — in industry as well as relationships and in work as well as hobbies. Taking notes on the best golfer you know really can help your game. The same is true of public speaking, negotiating, writing, or just about any pursuit. By noting how others have done things well (or not), you learn how to be successful yourself.

For example, Pittsburgh Steelers coach Mike Tomlin was hired at a very young age for a job as head coach in the National Football League. When he began having success very early in his head-coaching career, people started taking notice of his methods.

It soon became apparent that he had notebooks filled with observations he had handwritten over the years and that he consulted these notebooks on many occasions. People became curious and asked him about the notebooks.

It turned out that many years prior, while he was a young assistant coach in his first job for a college team, Tomlin started taking notes. He watched his coaches and wrote down many of their sayings, ideas, techniques, and philosophies that worked — along with those that didn't.

Over the years, he created quite a collection of notes: what to say during halftime in a number of situations and the results he could expect, what to do in tough situations and what to avoid, how to respond to a given circumstance in several different ways and the consequences of each response, and so on.

He hasn't made the notebooks public, so it's unclear exactly what wisdom they contain, but clearly Tomlin's attention to detail in watching how wiser and more experienced coaches did things — tracking the good and the not-so-good — is a real help to him now that he is in the top leadership role. (By the way, this works no matter how you feel about the Pittsburgh Steelers!)

You can do the same, in whatever field you work and in whatever arena you hope to earn success. Closely watch how leaders lead, what they do or don't do, and what they could have done, and write it all down for later reference. This is the powerful Drucker Principle of emulation.

In fact, Drucker suggested keeping written track of your *own* actions, schedules, projects, words, and techniques as well and referring to them later as needed.

The key to the Drucker Principle—effective emulation—is paying close attention, recording what leaders do, and using your notes to make your best choices when the time is right.

Three Benefits

This approach helps you develop a positive thick skin in at least three ways. First, when a challenge arises, you'll have the advantage of knowing what other leaders did or didn't do in similar circumstances and how things turned out. This is invaluable information.

Most people can't keep track of a bunch of such examples by memory, but your written notes can store hundreds of important thoughts and details. You'll have a thicker skin when you have the benefit of years of notes on what does and doesn't work.

Second, as you write the words and ideas of leaders, you'll invariably include quotes and thoughts that will be useful to you during times of difficulty. Reading quotes from a respected leader can help you calm yourself in a pinch and relax.

You'll make better decisions when the words and notes from leaders are part of your thinking, and you'll have more confidence in yourself and your choices—thus mitigating those naturally occurring self-doubts and worries that inevitably come when the stakes are high and all eyes are on you. The voices of mentors will help you choose well and stand strong—but only if you can remember what your mentors actually said.

> **You'll make better decisions when the words and notes from leaders are part of your thinking.**

Third, you'll get huge benefits just from experiencing how others lead. Especially if you are writing your thoughts with an eye toward learning from them later as a leader yourself, you'll learn a great deal about success, leadership, principles, and integrity.

Watching and listening to successful leaders, reading their words, and taking notes throughout can prepare you every day for successful leadership in your own life.

Ask any great leader where he or she learned his or her most important leadership lessons, and after mentioning how much he or she learned from his or her own mistakes, the leader will often share how much he or she gained directly and indirectly from the leadership of one or two people he or she admired. And if the leader took good notes, this learning was likely even better—probably much, much better.

Apply the effective emulation path to gaining a thick skin. Watch how good leaders do it, and take notes. Learn from their example, listen to their speeches and interviews, and read their writings. Above all, apply what they tell you.

Emulation works — because the leaders worth emulating only got there by learning how to succeed. Their lessons to you are invaluable. If you write those lessons down and reread them, they'll powerfully and positively thicken your skin (and enlighten your decision-making powers) when you need it most.

> **Above all, apply what good leaders tell you.**

5

THE EINSTEIN METHOD

THOUGHTS ARE THINGS

*Not snow, no, nor rain, nor heat, nor night keeps them from
accomplishing their appointed courses with all speed.*
— HERODOTUS

Albert Einstein famously taught that thoughts are things. This means that our thoughts are more than random, immaterial nothings. They are real. They are scientifically notable, they have real weight in our lives, and they impact our choices, feelings, emotions, and actions. Thoughts are things. Real things.

With that said, these real things we call thoughts can be helpful or hurtful. They can thin our skins to the point that we are tentative, wishy-washy, fickle, weak, and quickly swayed by other people who want to influence or even control us. This is the bad news about thoughts.

The good news is equally powerful: thoughts have real power. If we cultivate the right thoughts, they can make us strong, smart, energetic, wise, and successful. They can fill us with faith, motivate us to powerful action, and lead us to victory after victory in our journey to achieving our most cherished goals.

In short, our thoughts control us, but that's only half the story. The other half, the place of real power, is that we control our thoughts. If we reject the bad thoughts and continually choose and nurture the right thoughts, we can usher in a bright future.

> **Our thoughts control us, but that's only half the story. The other half, the place of real power, is that we control our thoughts.**

This doesn't mean that life will always be easy or devoid of challenges or that we can control the world like a genie in a bottle. It means that when we keep our thoughts on the right things in the right ways, we invite God's strength and use our faith to bring out the best we can be in this life.

When we don't control our thoughts properly, we become weak. But when we choose the right thoughts and continue to do so, we become powerful servants in God's hands. We do amazing things for good.

Getting our thinking right is incredibly powerful. Keeping our thinking right puts us on a powerful life purpose. Sticking with right thinking brings us great success and a lifetime of service—regardless of the obstacles and challenges we face. If we think about the right things in the right ways and stick to this, we become great leaders and do truly great things.

The Ant and the Elephant

Orrin Woodward likened this battle between the right thoughts and other thoughts (from bad to distracting to downright hurtful) to an ant running on the back of an elephant. Imagine that the elephant in this scenario is running in one direction, while the ant on the elephant's back is running in the opposite direction.

No matter how strong and focused the ant thoughts are, they'll never win. They're trying to go one direction, but the elephant thoughts are going so powerfully in the other direction that the ant thoughts are getting farther and farther behind.

For most people, the elephant thoughts are negative, and the ant thoughts are their attempts at being positive. Again, no matter how hard they try to keep positive thoughts going, the elephant power of their negative thoughts is moving too rapidly in the other direction.

In that way, the Einstein reality keeps most of us from ever getting ahead. Thoughts are things, and our negative thoughts are moving so strongly in one direction that our feeble attempts at the right thoughts just don't cover much ground. In fact, they're usually moving backward with the elephant's body, even as they try with all their might to move forward on his back. Sad, but true.

The Einstein Method is a solution to this dilemma. Since thoughts are things, real, palpable, actual things, we have more control over them than we might think. But to really get control of our thoughts, we've got to have a chat with the elephant—not just the ant.

The Project

The answer to this challenge is really quite ingenious. Orrin Woodward calls it Project 180°. In this project, he invites anyone who wants to be a real leader to get his or her subconscious mind (the elephant, so to speak) turned around and running in the same direction as the ant. This is tremendous medicine, if you can make it happen.

The key is to get the subconscious mind deeply focused on the positive, on the good things about you, your good ideas, your faith and dreams—not your doubt, worry, fear, anger, or self-criticism. Get the elephant turned around, and get both the elephant and the ant running in the same direction.

> **The key is to get the subconscious mind deeply focused on the positive.**

Easier said than done? Not if you know what to do.

Building on the Drucker Principle of emulating those who are true successes already, the Einstein Method involves immersing your brain in the words of the people you want to emulate. In short, some people have their elephant and ant both going in the right direction, working in tandem.

Who are these people? They are the ones who are experiencing the kind of success you want. That's why they're achieving the success—because their subconscious and conscious minds are fully aligned.

Woodward's amazing addition to this field is that it is possible to tap into this energy by simply immersing yourself in the thinking patterns of such people. To do this, Woodward teaches, read at least thirty minutes a day from the original words of people who are currently succeeding and whom you should be emulating (whose elephant thoughts are running in the right direction) and spend at least three hours a day listening to their recorded words and thoughts via audio.

If this sounds like too much, your negative elephant thoughts are quickly heading off in the wrong direction. You need to immerse yourself in the voices, words, thoughts, ideas, stories, and linguistic patterns of people whose elephant thoughts and subconscious minds are going the right way.

The longer you listen, the more your thoughts and brain patterns will start to align, the sooner your elephant will begin to turn around, and the more effectively your mind can get on the right track.

> **You need to immerse yourself in the voices, words, thoughts, ideas, stories, and linguistic patterns of people whose elephant thoughts and subconscious minds are going the right way.**

William's Experience

This is a powerful way to make the switch, and it really works. For example, when William first heard of Project

180°, he shrugged it off as just another speaker trying to sell a book. But when his nephew told him how much it had helped him, he decided to give it a try. "What can it hurt?" he asked himself.

The first day, he read for thirty minutes, got interested, and ended up reading for over an hour. He planned to cut the audios short, but after two hours, he was still interested and put on another one. He listened while he worked in his wood shop, and even though he didn't focus on every word or take notes, he found himself tuning in to the stories and sometimes zoning out to focus on something in his work or just to think.

That night, he told his wife that he had enjoyed the audios and book but didn't think they did anything special for him. But his nephew had let him borrow a whole box of CDs, so he kept listening for the rest of the week. By using his lunch breaks, he finished two-thirds of the book by Friday, and he was pleased that he'd had the information and ideas to think about all week. "Still no big change," he told his wife. "Just like I expected." (Oh, the power of the elephant thoughts!)

Then Saturday came. William spent the morning working with his three boys, digging fence-post holes and setting posts for a new horse field. They worked late into the afternoon, running wire around the field, and finally finished by setting the gate.

William took off his hat, rubbed the sweat from his brow, and smiled at his oldest son, Rob. "That was a good day," he said. "Mr. Twitchell will be glad we finished the whole fence today."

Rob nodded and took a long drink from his water bottle. Then he looked at his dad and asked, "Are you feeling okay today, Dad?"

"Why?" William asked.

"No reason. It's just that…well…you didn't yell at us once all day—not once. Usually you're pretty intense on these Saturday jobs. I know you like to get as much done as possible when all us boys are here to help, so you push and drive all day. Today you were…different."

"Really?" William was surprised. "In what way?"

"You were relaxed. We worked just as hard as every week, but you didn't yell. You didn't act driven. You just hummed, laughed, talked about our week, and shared stories from your childhood. Really, Dad, it was like working with a different person."

When William shared this with his wife later that evening, she nodded. "You've been that way for several days," she said. "It really is different."

"Wow," he replied. "I wonder why."

"It's the CDs!" she immediately said. "No doubt. I'm sure of it. I've been noticing the change for days. If you don't believe it, just stop listening and reading next week, and you'll be back to your, uh, intense self."

William pondered this and nodded slowly. "Huh! I guess it *could* be that. I think I'll do what you said and stop listening next week just to see if that's really it—"

"Don't you dare!" she said, with a big smile. "Please don't! Keep listening and reading. It's bringing out a better you. It really is."

William grinned. "I'll tell you what. I'll keep doing it if you'll start listening and reading as well. I've got all the CDs from last week, and you can play them in the background while you do your work online this week."

"That's a deal," she said.

This is a true story. Two months later, after continuing to read thirty or more minutes a day and listen to at least three hours a day of talks from people whose success was worth emulating, William and his wife had started a new business—inspired by their weeks of turning their elephant thoughts in the right direction. William's family members still comment on the major change in him.

The Real Critics

To make the change, William and his wife had to face and overcome years of thin-skinned choices. It turns out that they had been their own worst critics for a very long time. They had both been telling themselves lots of self-negatives and believing them.

"The elephant thoughts really had me believing the worst about myself," William said. "But now, after just a few weeks, I see myself and my future in a whole new light."

It's almost impossible to overcome thin-skin problems when your own brain is doing a bunch of the criticizing.

But the Einstein Method makes all the difference. Thoughts really are things, and the ant and the elephant are real.

The key to developing a positively thick skin is to begin by listening to the voices of people whose elephant thoughts are going in the right direction. Woodward's Project 180° combines the best tools of the Drucker Principle and the Einstein Method, and it is incredibly powerful.

> The key to developing a positively thick skin is to begin by listening to the voices of people whose elephant thoughts are going in the right direction.

An Invitation

Getting the elephant and the ant thoughts going the same direction will create your positive thick skin and start you on a path to more success in many, many ways. In short, get your subconscious (elephant) thoughts going in the right direction, and you'll move mountains. How? Immerse your thinking each day in the voices, writings, ideas, and words of people who are already moving their elephant in the right direction.

This is powerful mentoring, and it works! We invite you to start this project for yourself right away.

(To order a book and some audios to start on this powerful and effective process that can drastically improve your life, go to lifeleadership.com.)

6

THE EDISON PROCEDURE

RESTLESS AND RESPONSIVE

I have spoken. You have heard.
— ARISTOTLE

As we learned in the last chapter from the Einstein Method, one reason many people struggle with being thin-skinned is that they are their own worst critics. When the inner voices are constantly tearing you down, it's pretty hard to ever build or keep a positive thick skin.

> **When the inner voices are constantly tearing you down, it's pretty hard to ever build or keep a positive thick skin.**

It's like trying to fight a battle against an invading army from Mordor when you have Orc spies inside your castle who keep opening the gates for the enemy. Not a very effective strategy!

Of course, Project 180° can get that turned around in a surprising hurry. But then, once you stop letting negative elephant thoughts undermine your success and progress, it is essential to replace the void of old negative thoughts with a lot of new, powerful, effective thoughts.

Actually, when you stop listening to the negatives, you'll probably be amazed at how many positive thoughts you've had in your mind all along! This brings us to the Edison Procedure.

Discontent Breeds Action, and Action Breeds Change

The truth is that many of the ongoing thoughts in your mind aren't negative at all. They're positive. Some of your daily positive thoughts are the uplifting, relaxed, happy kinds of thoughts most of us wish would dominate our every waking (and sleeping) moment. These kinds of positive, happy thoughts are wonderful.

But, in fact, there is another kind of positive thought pattern that is even more helpful. We'll call this kind of thinking by the delightful term *restless thoughts*.

Everyone has them, but the secret is that truly successful leaders have more of them than most people. Why? Because top leaders have realized that restless thoughts are on the positive side of the ledger, not the negative, and that they are actually among the most powerful thoughts of all.

Top leaders do shut down any negative thoughts, focusing on keeping the elephant going in the right direction, but they've learned that restless thoughts are the best kind of positive thoughts.

What does all this mean? Only that a positively restless man or woman is ready to do important things. This makes a person hungry for positive progress: motivated, willing to make changes and do hard things, and poised to respond.

As the great Thomas Edison put it, "Restlessness is discontent — and discontent is the first necessity of progress. Show me a thoroughly satisfied man — and I will show you a failure."[1]

> "Restlessness is discontent — and discontent is the first necessity of progress. Show me a thoroughly satisfied man — and I will show you a failure."
> —Thomas Edison

Three Kinds of People

This quotation also introduces us to the three kinds of people in the world. First, we have the people who are led through life by their many negative thoughts. They frequently work hard and try to do good, but they experience few great successes. Their *Orc thoughts* just keep opening the gates to their enemies, blocking them from truly living their dreams.

You don't want to be an Orc because all your efforts just never seem to bring you what you really want. This is sad. Robert Kiyosaki called this spending your life in the "rat race" — working hard, trying, giving your all, but never getting what you want.

Why? Because your negative Orc thoughts don't let you turn your efforts into true achievements. Your Orc thoughts consistently hold you back.

When a person figures out how to stop the negative thoughts, turn the elephant around, and start in the right direction, the next challenge is to struggle with *dwarf thoughts*. This is the second kind of person.

In their new focus on positive thinking, many people mistake their restless thoughts for negative thoughts and throw them out. They don't realize that these restless thoughts are actually positive, that they are really allies, not enemies.

They get caught in fantasy thinking, only dwelling on the easy, relaxed, fluffy positive thoughts. The result is what Edison called being too content, feeling "thoroughly satisfied," not allowing positive restless feelings to motivate them to the hard work of real change and powerful action.

You don't want to get caught up in negative Orc thinking or weak dwarf fantasizing. Real leaders push past both of these ineffective thought patterns. They learn to get the elephant going in the right direction, to replace negative thoughts with all positives.

> **Real leaders push past ineffective thought patterns.**

But they don't stop there. They also learn that the right kind of Edison restless thoughts are truly positive and amazingly motivating. They become the third kind of people: *elves*.

Such people learn to stay away from negative thoughts, enjoy the uplifting kind of happy positive thoughts, and allow their restless thoughts to help them consider, choose, do, and accomplish great things. This is profound and powerful.

Thicker by the Day

But how does this relate to getting and keeping a positive thick skin that will help you be a much better leader? Answer: Implementing the Edison Procedure simply means you always sort and control your thoughts in three ways:

1. Throw out negative thoughts.
2. Enjoy happy positive thoughts.
3. But also live and bask in restless thoughts, and write them down!

This is huge! Really successful people — the ones who are worthy of watching and emulating (the Drucker Principle) and listening to and following, so as to immerse yourself in the right kind of powerful leadership thinking (the Einstein Method) — learn to master the Edison Procedure. They get the elephant and the ant going in the right direction, and then they allow positive restless thoughts to help them get excited about doing great things that will effectively bring real, lasting change.

Go Restless!

Specifically, top leaders gain a positive thick skin by focusing *in a specific way* on the positives instead of the negatives. Drucker said the key to success is to "starve the problems" and "feed the opportunities."[2]

But great leaders don't just spend their days fighting with their own thoughts, beating down negatives and happily picturing fluffy positive thoughts floating around in front of their eyes like white clouds. They don't count sheep or flick themselves with the rubber bands on their wrists every time a negative thought comes along. They have another way of dealing with all this, a more natural way — a more effective way.

> Top leaders gain a positive thick skin by focusing *in a specific way* on the positives instead of the negatives.

They apply the Edison Procedure. In short, great leaders do consciously work to downplay negative thoughts and fill their minds with positives. They work hard to make sure they always keep the elephant going in the right direction. But they are helped in this battle in a huge way: they spend most of their waking hours deeply, passionately focused on achieving their dreams! And such dreams are *always* achieved at the expense of the status quo. This is why fostering restlessness is so important.

Such restless souls go after their goals. They spend their days and nights on this, giving their hearts to their life purpose. They let the restless thoughts in their lives help them dream bigger, plan better, and execute more effectively.

They wake up excited to jump out of bed and get on with their day. Why? Because they are excited by their goals, projects, and work. Deeply excited. Passionately dedicated.

They smile first thing in the morning when what first pops into their mind is their dreams and how their work today will help make their dreams a reality.

Positive Thinking Multiplied

Their dreams and goals drive them and fill them with passion, enthusiasm, and seemingly boundless energy. When they experience negatives, they put them aside and focus on positives.

When they feel happy and relaxed, they smile and enjoy the mood, but they don't let it take over. They use moments of peace and relaxation to open their creative minds and ask, "How can I do better? What more can I do to really make a difference? How can I improve my life? Myself? The world? How can I help others?"

These are Edison's restless thoughts, and they are incredibly important. Top leaders bask in such thoughts, always considering ways to improve today and the world—for themselves and for others. They don't just keep the elephant going in the right direction; they ride it to get where they want to go—to achieve their goals, to earn their dreams, to live their God-given purpose and mission in life.

With these concerns dominating their thoughts, they don't have time for thin skin. They're too busy. They're just plain focused on something else, not on negatives, and not even on mere positives.

They live on positive alert, excited by the next challenge and opportunity, ready at a moment's notice to smile more broadly and go to work improving themselves, their business, their career, their relationships, and anything else in the world that comes to mind.

> **Whenever they experience a restless thought, top leaders immediately get to work putting positive changes and upgrades into place.**

They unleash their creativity on the world, always grabbing onto the latest restless sense that something could be better. Whenever they experience a restless thought, they immediately think about it, brainstorm, imagine, plan, call their friends to discuss, and get to work putting positive changes and upgrades into place.

Their minds are never idle, so the negatives can't get a foothold. They give a foothold only to restless ideas about what needs to be improved, solved, enhanced, and perfected.

Then, routinely, elves (top leaders) turn such restless thoughts into important, well-considered responses. This is the Edison Procedure, where the "light bulb in the brain never goes off," and it does a lot more than replace negatives with positives. It replaces the status quo with a vision for what can be.

It's not just positive mental attitude. It's positive effort to change the world—now, later, tomorrow, always.

When you are constantly thinking about how to better everything, especially matters in your area of stewardship, a thick skin is the natural side effect of being so focused on the truly important stuff that what's shallow just melts away in comparison. You simply don't have the bandwidth to be bothered by the criticism of those who are not part of what you're trying to accomplish.

A Pen and a Brain

How can you follow this pattern? The truth is it's easy. The challenging part is to learn and apply the Drucker Principle and the Einstein Method. Once you're doing both of these consistently, the Edison Procedure is simple.

Here's what you do: Anytime you feel a sense of restlessness about something that needs to be fixed, something that's not quite right (a relationship, an upcoming speech, a system at the office, a concern you recently discussed with the executive team or the board, or something that is just a little off) get out a pen, a blank piece of paper, and your brain.

Brainstorm ways to improve what's bothering you. To solve problems. To jump on an opportunity. To heal a relationship. To fix a system. Brainstorm, and write down your thoughts. Don't wait for plans; just write down ideas. Don't analyze each one; just get them all on paper. Get as many ideas on paper as you can.

When you're tapped out, when no more ideas are coming, shift gears. Now start thinking about each one, which will work and which won't. Circle or underline great ideas and notes that might really help. Cross out any that just won't work.

Spend time with this: just your pen, paper, and brain — and heart. This will bring out the restless thoughts, the Edison power, and the thoughts will come fast and furious. Or you'll jump straight to the "one big thought" that makes all the difference.

A positively thick skin keeps us focused on what is truly important, so that our restlessness and creative responses can emphasize the right things — the real things, the things that matter most. Actually, the opposite is also true: when we inspire ourselves to stick to what really deserves our attention, we grow a thicker skin. This can — and should — become a habit.

> When we inspire ourselves to stick to what really deserves our attention, we grow a thicker skin. This can — and should — become a habit.

Don't skip this step. It is powerful. It works. The Edison Procedure is real. It gets the best thoughts out of your mind and onto the paper. Once they're in front of you, you can grapple with and think about each idea.

If you want to be a great leader, to tap into your best wisdom and creativity and leadership, learn to attune your mind (and pen hand) to solving real challenges and engaging great opportunities. Not only will this make you positively thick-skinned, it will turn you into a top leader.

In short, whenever you feel any sense of restlessness, grab your pen and start brainstorming and writing!

This is your brain on paper!

Thank you, Mr. Edison.

PART III

FOUR MORE POWERFUL HELPS

Few men speak humbly of humility.

—BLAISE PASCAL

7

THE QUARTERBACK TECHNIQUE

A SHORT MEMORY OF THE RIGHT KIND

Rule No. 11: When the job is done, walk away.
—GIBBS FROM *NCIS*

If you've learned and are applying the Drucker Principle (emulate the right people), the Einstein Method (read and listen to the words of the right mentors for at least three hours a day to get your brain patterns going in the right direction), and the Edison Procedure (use pen and paper to brainstorm, write down, and plan—every time you experience anything except easy, fun, fluffily happy thoughts and feelings), you're on the path to great leadership. Your skin is positively thickening even as you read this. Great achievements are ahead for you. Nothing will stop you if you keep it up.

If fact, if you stop reading right now and only continue to effectively apply these three important techniques, you will become a great leader. You don't need the rest of this book to do that. We could just end the book right here, but there are four additional little things that can really help you in your journey. They aren't absolutely necessary, but they are very handy. And since change, leadership, and greatness can be the hardest undertakings in life, every little advantage helps.

> **If you've learned and are applying the Drucker Principle, the Einstein Method, and the Edison Procedure, you're on the path to great leadership.**

So we're going to share them with you because they are so useful. Just remember that these four additional tools won't do you much good if you're not using the Drucker Principle, the Einstein Method, and the Edison Procedure.

If you are implementing all three of these powerful approaches, the four tools in the rest of this book will greatly improve your effectiveness both in maintaining a positive thick skin and in becoming a truly great leader. Plus, they're fun.

"Red, Forty-One, Omaha, Hut, Hut, Hike!"

The first of the four tools is the Quarterback Technique. Leadership is all about mission and life purpose. It isn't enough to become skilled at responding to the bumps, bruises, and pains of a thin skin. Great leaders need to be truly thick-skinned, to listen only to the right voices.

They need to be humble, sure, focused, and receptive to genuine, constructive criticism that provides opportunities for improvement. But they must not become shackled, distracted, or oversensitive.

In the National Football League, there is a concept known as "a bad short-term memory." This trait is considered absolutely essential for any good quarterback. At first, this may seem counterintuitive for most people. "Why would anyone want a *bad* short-term memory?" you might ask. "Wouldn't a *good* memory be better?"

Maybe it would, in some cases. But not for quarterbacks. And not for most other leaders, either. A bad short-term memory is the real goal.

Think about it. A professional quarterback has to lead his team against eleven of the fastest, strongest, biggest, and most athletically talented men in the world, trying to push them out of the way and move the ball all the way down the field. This is hard. No matter how good you are, when facing this level of opposition, you're going to lose some. You'll win some, if you're good enough, but you'll lose some as well.

When a great quarterback loses, once, twice, or maybe even eight times in a row, he (or she) has to forget all the mistakes of the last eight tries and approach the next drive like it's the first. Fresh. Enthusiastic. Confident. Ready.

You can't dwell on the mistakes that led to failure the previous eight times — even though they just happened during the last hour. You have to forget them, put them in the past, and positively focus on the very next play. (This could be called the Great Sales Technique as well as the Quarterback Technique.)

One Example

This kind of enthusiastic focus on the next move – while forgetting the last eight or twenty mistakes as if they'd never happened – takes a special kind of leadership. You have to have a short memory.

Steve Young had such a memory. Young once led his team to a crushing defeat after throwing four interceptions in a major loss in Atlanta. After the game, the head coach, worried that his young quarterback would be depressed and overwhelmed and not prepare well for the next game ahead, asked Steve how he was feeling. He responded that it had been such a great game, so much fun!

> He knew he had a winner on his hands. Why? Because of his attitude: short memory about the mistakes, long memory about his purpose and goals.

His coach immediately knew he had a winner leading his team. He couldn't know at that early date that Steve would become a Super Bowl champion or an NFL Hall of Fame quarterback, but he knew he had a winner on his hands. Why? Because of his attitude: short memory about the mistakes, long memory about his purpose and goals.

Telling the Difference

Note that when people have an attitude of winning with a bad short-term memory about mistakes, they can be either (1) just naïve and deluded or (2) great leaders. The difference is that naïve people aren't following the Drucker Principle, the Einstein Method, and the Edison Procedure, so all their positive mental thinking is just delusion.

But those who are applying the lessons of Drucker, Einstein, and Edison are using their positive attitude to create a powerful atmosphere of leadership. They are creating an environment of winning and success.

Add the right kind of short-term memory to someone applying these important principles, and he or she becomes a resilient, enthusiastic, excellent leader. Like the best NFL quarterbacks, all great leaders benefit by strengthening the habits of a short memory — quickly fixing what needs to be fixed and then effectively putting mistakes and negatives behind them. This leads to a focus on truly excelling in today's opportunities.

Living in the past, worrying about the future, or allowing distraction right now — these are the classic symptoms of having a thin skin. Positive thick-skinned leadership means putting the past in the past, learning from mistakes in positive ways, and then moving on!

Flipside

We can look at this a little deeper. While one side of the coin is to quickly forget mistakes and focus instead on the positive, the other side is the opposite: don't read your press clippings.

No matter how well you did at something, there is always something you could have done better.

> "Find a defeat in every victory... and a victory in every defeat."
> —Orrin Woodward

Perhaps Orrin Woodward puts the two together best when he says to "find a defeat in every victory (to improve) and a victory in every defeat (to maintain morale)."[1] It is from such a mindset that we can find the steady middle-ground mentality of a champion.

8

THE C. S. LEWIS APPROACH

BE AN ORIGINAL

Critics are spectators.
— CHRIS BRADY

A fifth key to developing a truly positive thick skin is
to be yourself, to be authentically you. This is oft-re-
peated advice, but it is too rarely applied. Most people
take conformity in life, school, and career much too far,
and in the process, they forget to be themselves.

As Chris Brady writes in the bestselling book *Rascal*,
the way to truly make a difference in the world is "by
becoming an original character." Such characters, Brady
says, "are known by what they do. Their unique character
produces fruit different from that of the vast majority of
people."[1]

Brady then quotes the 1928 Broadway musical *The
New Moon*:

Give me some men
Who are Stout-Hearted Men
Who will fight for the right they adore
Start me with ten
Who are Stout-Hearted Men
And I'll soon give you ten thousand more
Shoulder to shoulder, and bolder and bolder
They grow as they go to the fore...[2]

This summarizes the essence of being yourself. You are unique, and when you let your best self shine the results are, ironically, downright contagious. Other people see your unique character and want to be like you. The word for such behavior is, simply, *leadership*.

It turns out that almost everyone wants to be a unique, strong leader. They just need someone to show them how and to lead out!

> **Almost everyone wants to be a unique, strong leader. They just need someone to show them how and to lead out!**

Those who succeed in their life purpose always, *always* follow the path of wise submission to mentors and leaders who have already fruitfully walked the road and know what to do (and avoid). Then they take an important step beyond the Drucker Principle: not only do they learn from those who have proven success in what they are seeking, but they learn to do it their *own* best way.

They combine wise principles with their own unique strengths, talents, skills, and abilities. They focus on their strengths, not their weaknesses, and they mix these strengths with the best techniques, attitudes, and principles taught by successful mentors. In short, they learn and then master the rules of the game; then they set about redefining the game entirely.

> **Those who succeed in their life purpose learn and then master the rules of the game; then they set about redefining the game entirely.**

Men without Chests

The humility to submit to the right mentor(s) is a vital trait of success. The dumbed-down popular views of how to succeed in your mission—the reality TV version of "wisdom"—are mostly a waste of time. Only those who have walked the path and truly earned success can effectively mentor those who seek to do it even better.

Today's leaders build on the shoulders of giants, while the "other 95 percent" persist in the false mythology that there is an easy way or one path for everyone and that the best mentors are credentialed experts. But that's the rub. Just copying other leaders will never make you a leader.

As C. S. Lewis described it, "We make men without chests and expect of them virtue and enterprise. We laugh at honour

> **"We make men without chests and expect of them virtue and enterprise. We laugh at honour and are shocked to find traitors in our midst. We castrate and bid the geldings be fruitful."**
> **—C. S. Lewis**

and are shocked to find traitors in our midst. We castrate and bid the geldings be fruitful."[3]

In truth, the best mentors are usually what Malcolm Gladwell called the entrepreneurial "outliers" or what C. S. Lewis referred to as the true "master craftsmen." These are people who aren't trying to impress the world but rather to accomplish their great purpose in life.

In other words, *you should learn not only from mentors who actually have what you want to achieve but also from mentors who are positively thick-skinned, who don't care about what others think of them because they are too focused on the importance of their life work.*

Be a Trailblazer

Such mentors are Alvin Toffler's outside-the-box visionaries and trendsetters who reject the rote and add their personality to their work and service. They are Emerson's self-reliant pioneers, trailblazers, and innovators who personalize and individualize their best service to every person they lead.

They aren't focused on what people think; they are focused on what is actually important. They have the guts—what C. S. Lewis called the "chest"—or heart to be unique, original leaders.

> In short, to have a thick skin, you need to learn to be comfortable in your own skin.

In short, to have a thick skin, you need to learn to be comfortable in your own skin. Consider the great basketball player

Michael Jordan, who, when told by a journalist what an opponent had said about him, looked at the reporter in surprise and wanted to know why he should care about that. His heart, thoughts, and goals were focused on winning, and he simply didn't care what someone else had to say.

Likewise, we can all learn from the old mountain man in Wyoming who was falsely accused of a crime and eventually found not guilty by the jury. When his attorney, the famous Gerry Spence, told him he was sorry for all the things critics were saying about him in the newspaper, the man looked quizzically at his lawyer and said simply, "I'm free." He didn't care a bit what anyone thought or said.

Guts Matter

Again, this kind of positive thick skin is rare, but it is powerful. The higher people rise as leaders, the more they learn to adopt such a thick skin. Without it, they'll stop progressing. "Leadership is lonely," Orrin Woodward says, "because there are always people wanting to look down on you even though you're climbing the ladder of leadership and they're not."

When you *do* climb the ladder of leadership, you learn to respect other authentic leaders — who face the gauntlet of criticism and even haters and just keep focusing on their important life purpose. This is a requirement of real success.

When You're "All Cattle," No Hat Is Needed

The path of leadership is so much easier, and more effective, when you simultaneously follow the wisdom of successful mentors and also stay true to yourself. Being "an original character," or even a bit of a "Rascal," as Chris Brady puts it, is vital for building a positive thick skin, and it is also crucial in becoming a real leader.

Top leaders are never clones or posers. They are always genuine originals. They learn to be comfortable in their skin and to be themselves — their *best* selves.

There is an old Texas saying that some people are "all hat, no cattle." This means they have a nice, big cowboy hat, the kind typically afforded by men of substance and success, but they don't have the substance or the success — they're just trying to put forth the *appearance* of success.

In truth, it's a lot better to be "all cattle, no hat." When you are genuinely impressive as a person and leader (when your actions and results do the impressing), you don't have to try to impress. You just go out and do your thing.

That's incredibly impressive. And, honestly, it's the *only* thing that actually is impressive, as C. S. Lewis described in his article entitled "The Inner Ring."[4] And it allows you to focus on your real purpose.

This is the blessing of a positive thick skin, and it is an essential trait of every great leader. So apply the C. S. Lewis Approach in your life, work, and relationships by being yourself — but only and always your best self.

Yes, learn to improve yourself as much as possible. And certainly learn from the right mentors. In addition, be unique. Be real. Be genuine. Otherwise, as C. S. Lewis taught, you'll waste most of your life trying to be something less than you could be in the hope that other shallow people will accept you.

That's not a good life or path. Your life is meant for much better things! As Janelle Monáe put it, "Embrace the things that make you unique, even if it makes people uncomfortable."[5]

9

THE CHURCHILL QUESTIONS

"WHO IS YOUR TEAM?" AND "WHO ARE YOUR ALLIES?"

We shall not flag or fail. We shall go on to the end....
We shall never surrender.
—WINSTON CHURCHILL

One of the greatest decisions leaders make was exemplified by Winston Churchill and can be summarized by the two questions above. The right team and the right allies thicken our skin in broad and deep ways. Show us a person's genuine friends, and we'll show you his or her capacity (or lack of it) to sway the world and the future.

Top leaders don't succeed alone. They do it with a team, with a committed and proven group of companions who together work, sacrifice, support, adjust, adapt, and overcome whatever challenges arise. The idea of the lone great leader is always a shallow telling of the true story—where the greatest accomplishments resulted from the efforts of a band of dedicated comrades working together for a great cause.

The single "man on the white horse" theory of leadership is almost always false. George Washington, Abraham Lincoln, Andrew Carnegie, Winston Churchill, Margaret Thatcher, Steve Jobs—successful leaders *always* have a team of colleagues.

For example, Churchill was the great leader of World War II, but without the right team and allies, he would have lost. He'd have gone down in history as a major failure, the man who let Nazism and tyranny conquer his nation and much of the world.

Instead, fortunately, Churchill knew he needed an excellent team and great allies in order to win, and he went out of his way to work with them effectively.

The Team Approach

Great leaders know to link arms with the right people and turn their cooperation and even competition into a team effort. Devoted teams generate exponentially more synergy, strength, wisdom, resilience, excellence, and unswerving tenacity than any man or woman can ever produce alone.

> Devoted teams generate exponentially more synergy, strength, wisdom, resilience, excellence, and unswerving tenacity than any man or woman can ever produce alone.

Just think about this list of powerful words: *synergy, strength, wisdom, resilience, excellence*, and *unswerving tenacity*. Add these together and combine them with a group of leaders working together—instead of alone—and you have a true formula for lasting success. This kind of teamwork is what changes the world.

Churchill would never have won World War II without a small, dedicated team of strong leaders in the Parliament, the Cabinet, the government, and the military. He also broadened his team to include key leaders in academia, the media, finance, and industry. Without these relationships and combined efforts, Britain's efforts would have been doomed.

Effective leaders apply this same team principle in their business, department, company, family, and other circles.

The Outlier Approach

In addition to a great core team of colleagues, really successful leaders also build strong friendships and relationships with outlying leaders—people who aren't part of the everyday team but show the same caliber in their own life purpose. It's not enough to be part of a great team; real leaders also have some high-quality friends in various walks of life whose allies they can become when the need arises.

For Churchill, this meant reaching beyond the borders of his own nation and creating effective relationships and alliances with top leaders beyond the scope of his own leadership. Without such connections in France, Canada, the United States, and elsewhere, Churchill and his team of dedicated British leaders would have lost the conflict.

The United States, Canada, and Russia stepped up and helped to save Churchill and his nation in their time of greatest need.

> **Great leaders know how to build solid, powerful relationships even with people they don't specifically lead.**

It isn't always easy to work with people outside your own leadership circle, as Churchill found in dealing with Roosevelt and others, but it is an essential trait of great leaders. They know how to build solid, powerful relationships even with people they don't specifically lead.

Combined Thickness

Both kinds of allies (internal and external) are invaluable, and they add incredible strength when a leader or a cause is attacked, maligned, or challenged in any way. When you run into criticism and the immediate response

> **Earning and keeping the respect of those you respect is a hundred times more powerful than the chirps of posers and pretenders.**

is strong support from those you lead and work with every day—and also from other, independent leaders who know you personally and risk themselves to stand up for your integrity and character—you have a thicker skin. Period. Earning and keeping the respect of those you respect is a hundred times more powerful than the chirps of posers and pretenders.

Also, consider this whole matter from another angle. From the viewpoint of the people doing the sniping or attacking, your combined positive thick-skinned "meter" is measured not just in terms of your personal actions but also by the united strength of your team and colleagues as well. Add to this the power of outside friends and allies who jump to your defense, and the attacker sees a solid, powerful wall of strength. This feels like a lot more than skin — it's as thick as a brick wall. This is an excellent place to be as a leader.

Make Your Skin as Thick as a Brick Wall!

It only happens this way when you genuinely earn it, when you are the kind of leader and friend with the integrity that makes other people want to stand with you in the face of challenges. You have to live it, being the kind of person and ally who is worthy of such support, long before any difficulty comes.

In truth, with the right allies — internal as well as external to your leadership — you are always much, much stronger than even you might think or know. This is powerful!

One of the greatest experiences of leadership is to be attacked and respond in your quiet moments alone with human concern and even hurt or worry but then see a near avalanche of support sweep in from those you lead and also from other, outside leaders who voluntarily take a stand for you. Now *that's* leadership!

The support of allies doesn't take the place of the Drucker Principle, the Einstein Method, or the Edison

Procedure, but it certainly helps! In fact, if you are doing these three things and the others discussed in these pages, the additional support of team members and allies will be a massive help. The Churchill Questions are a great part of true leadership.

Just ask yourself: "Who is my team, and who are our allies?" If you need to do better in building both, take action now. This is an exceptional leadership decision. Of course, don't do it in order to have friends when challenges come. Do it in order to have friends and to help them. That's real friendship and real leadership.

10

THE LEADERSHIP WAY

SERVICE IS DESTINY

Let us die, and rush into the heart of the fight.
—Virgil

Ultimately, as every great leader learns, it's all about service. Those who make the world better are great. Those who don't, aren't. This is leadership in a nutshell. It boils down to the quality of your service in life.

What a leader transmits to the world—and how the world transmits this into the future—determines the direction of current and upcoming generations. In short, service is destiny.

Whatever value men or women add to the world, this is their legacy. And life is ultimately about contribution

> **Your success will be determined mostly by your contributions, not your achievements.**

more than achievement. This bears repeating: Your success will be determined mostly by your contributions, not your achievements. In fact, your contributions will largely *determine* your achievements.

Character Trumps Reputation

Character always trumps reputation, and genuine service always trumps the trappings of success. Gandhi said, "The best way to find yourself is to lose yourself in the service of others."[1] Our life purpose and mission are only as good as how well we bless the world, and when the mission is the thing, the ego and its sensitive thin skin lose importance. As Emily Dickinson wrote of service:

> If I can stop one Heart from breaking
> I shall not live in vain
> If I can ease one Life the Aching
> Or cool one Pain[2]

This is another great addition to becoming positively thick-skinned: Choose a life of service. When you do this, when you spend your life caring about others and helping them succeed, what matters is the service.

If your service succeeds, you won't care what anyone thinks or says about you. If your service succeeds, you'll know you've been truly successful. When your service succeeds, you'll smile and feel genuine happiness, knowing you're doing what you were born to do.

This is the apex of success, the zenith of living: knowing that you've fulfilled your God-given purpose in life — knowing you've done it! This is the goal.

> **This is the apex of success, the zenith of living: knowing that you've fulfilled your God-given purpose in life.**

Nothing else comes close to this feeling. Nothing else comes close to this kind of triumph. Beyond all the hard work, all the effort, all the trying — this is what it's all about.

The Journey

But we don't have to wait to complete our life purpose to enjoy this feeling. It's not just the destination; we can experience these same feelings all along the journey. How? By simply asking ourselves, today, "Am I fully living my life purpose right now? Am I doing it?"

If the answer is "Yes," you are on track! Your work matters! You matter! Your service matters! And you are doing it. That's the key to success: to know and feel this every day.

If the answer is ever "No, I need to do more or to do better," then even this is great. Now you'll know you need to improve. Figure out what you need to do better, or more of, and get to work on it! Immediately!

A Day in the Life of a Leader

This is how great leaders live their days. "Am I fully living my life purpose right now? Yes? Wonderful! I love my life! I love these people I'm serving. I love to serve. I love my work. This is so fun!"

Or, alternatively, "Am I fully living my life purpose right now? No? Okay, what do I need to do better? What do I need to do more of? I'll pull out a pen and a piece of paper and write down what I need to do. Then I'll do it. This will put me right on track for greatness! This is so exciting! I'm starting *right now*."

Day after day after day, this process creates great leaders. Those who don't follow it? They have to learn to settle for mediocrity — or at least something less than their very best life of truly great service in a powerful purpose that matters more than anything else.

But you don't want to settle.

You want to rise to your best. You want to achieve the greatness God put in you, the greatness God wants you to reach for and earn through daily service. With His help and your hard work, you'll do it.

When you do, even for one day, you'll know you're on track. This is leadership. And by the way, when this is your focus, your service and the people you serve and the life purpose you're working for are just too important to let you get sidetracked by a thin skin. You'll be way too immersed in doing the great things God has for you to work on today.

Talk about leadership! This is where it really takes off, when you focus on the real reason for today: your true service.

AN INVITATION TO FIND YOUR WAY

The future depends on what we do in the present.

—GANDHI

When it comes to being a great leader and focusing on the powerful service you have to offer the world, the seven little keys in this book can help. To recap:

1. **The Drucker Principle**: Seek out and follow the advice and examples of people who have what you want and have achieved what you want to achieve.

2. **The Einstein Method**: Use the power of thoughts by engaging Project 180° and immersing your brain for at least three and a half hours a day in the words, voices, thought patterns, and teachings of people who have achieved what you want. Get your thinking moving in the right direction.

3. **The Edison Procedure**: At least weekly (and more often is great), get out a pen and blank paper and

brainstorm and plan the things you need to do to really excel right now; write them down and do them. *Do them!*

4.   **The Quarterback Technique**: Develop a short memory of the right kind by learning the important lessons from each mistake and then forgetting the mistake, permanently putting it behind you and quickly moving on with enthusiasm and confidence.

5.   **The C. S. Lewis Approach**: Get strong by being yourself, combining the principles of success you learn from the right mentors with your unique, one-of-a-kind personality. Be yourself, improve yourself, and be your *best* self!

6.   **The Churchill Questions**: Build a great team and work with your team members to make a positive difference in the world, and also build great friendships with outside leaders who are doing great things as well. Both kinds of relationships will drastically increase the level and quality of your efforts. Your achievements will be significantly leveraged and increased by your positive relationships with team members and outside allies.

7.   **The Leadership Way**: Always remember that service is destiny and that real success is not about you but about helping those you serve and giving your all each day to fully build your God-given life purpose.

Take Action Now

These seven principles will make all the difference between a life of great success and...anything less. If you apply them and master them, you'll become a great leader. As you help others do the same, you'll become a builder of leaders — and together with other leaders, you'll do great things to improve the world.

The truth is the world is in desperate need of more leaders. Just watch the news tonight, any night, and see how much leadership is lacking in so many ways. The world needs you.

As you apply these seven techniques, you'll develop a positively thick skin, the kind that allows you to skim past the inevitable critics and not get distracted, the kind that helps you stay focused on what really matters.

In truth, the world needs what only you can offer. We need your unique, even strange blend of character, integrity, leadership, grit, wisdom, and dreams. Nobody can replace you, and if you fall short of your leadership greatness, the whole world will be the less for it.

These seven powerful principles will make you a great leader if you learn them, apply them, and live them. Each strengthens the other six, and together, the seven are a powerful formula for great

> **The world needs what only you can offer.**

leadership. We invite you to commit yourself to the leadership path, to reach for your very best.

Will there be challenges and critics along the way? Of course. But that is just the reality of leadership. The real question is much more valuable: Are you going to settle for some level of mediocrity in your life or reach for — and achieve — the very best you have to give?

We know you are up to the challenge. We know you have greatness in your future, if you choose to follow the path of leadership. We also know that applying these seven principles will make the path easier, simpler, and a lot more fun. So get started now.

If you've never considered becoming a leader, make the choice to do it. If you're already working on your leadership goals, keep going! Don't let anything stand in your way.

Put on the Uniform

Whatever your current situation and whatever your future goals, apply these seven principles of leadership. They will help you reach the highest level of your potential. They will help you serve and bless the lives of many people. They will help you fully achieve your great life purpose.

Above all, they will help you serve others every day, and in the process, you will become truly great. So if the uniform of leadership truly is thick skin, it's time you put it on!

NOTES

Introduction

1 Sean Woods, "Robert Reich on Inequality," *Men's Journal*, November 2013, copyright 2014 Men's Journal LLC, www.mensjournal.com/magazine/robert-reich-on-inequality-20131022.

2 Chris Brady and Orrin Woodward, *LIFE*, Second Edition (Flint, MI: Obstaclés Press, 2013), p.144.

Chapter 1: The Leadership Surprise

1 Claude Hamilton, *Toughen Up!* (Flint, MI: Obstaclés Press, 2013), p.77-78.

2 Ibid., p. 78-79.

Chapter 2: The Universal Search for Admiration

1 Bill Walsh with Steve Jamison and Craig Walsh, *The Score Takes Care of Itself: My Philosophy of Leadership* (New York: Portfolio, The Penguin Group, 2009).

Chapter 3: The Four Allegiances

1 Orrin Woodward, Twitter status, October 17, 2013 at 9:13 a.m., https://twitter.com/Orrin_Woodward/status/390873098263998464.

Chapter 4: The Drucker Principle

1 Oliver DeMille, *A Thomas Jefferson Education: Teaching a Generation of Leaders for the Twenty-First Century* (The Leadership Education Library Book 1) (Cedar City, UT: George Wythe College Press, 2006).

2 Chris Brady, *A Month of Italy: Rediscovering the Art of Vacation* (Flint, MI: Obstaclés Press, 2012).

3 Austin Kleon, *Steal Like an Artist: 10 Things Nobody Told You about Being Creative* (New York: Workman Publishing Company Inc., 2012), p. 36.

Chapter 6: The Edison Procedure

1 *The Diary and Sundry Observations of Thomas Alva Edison*, edited by Dagobert D. Runes (Abbey Publishing, 1968), www.goodreads.com/quotes/191354-restlessness-is-discontent-and-discontent-is-the-first-necessity.

2 Peter F. Drucker, *The Effective Executive* (New York: Harper Business Essentials, 2002), p. 98 and 171.

Chapter 7: The Quarterback Technique

1 Orrin Woodward, *RESOLVED: 13 Resolutions for LIFE*, Second Edition (Flint, MI: Obstaclés Press, 2012), p. 132. See also, Orrin Woodward, *RESOLVED Primer* (Flint, MI: Obstaclés Press, 2012), p. 69.

Chapter 8: The C. S. Lewis Approach

1 Chris Brady, *Rascal: Making a Difference by Becoming an Original Character*, Second Edition (Flint, MI: Obstaclés Press, 2012), p. 22.

2 Ibid., p. 23.

3 C. S. Lewis, *The Abolition of Man* (New York: HarperCollins Publishers, 2001), p. 26.

4 C. S. Lewis's "The Inner Ring" was the Memorial Lecture at King's College, University of London, in 1944, www.lewissociety.org/innerring.php.

5 Chris Azzopardi, "EXCLUSIVE: Janelle Monáe Q&A: The Gay Interview," *PrideSource*, originally published 9/12/2013 (Issue 2137, *Between The Lines News*), www.pridesource.com/article.html?article=62186.

Chapter 10: The Leadership Way

1 Mohandas Karamchand Gandhi/Mahatma Gandhi, as quoted in "12 Great Quotes from Gandhi on His Birthday" by Ashoka, *Forbes*, posted October 2, 2012 at 11:55 a.m., www.forbes.com/sites/ashoka/2012/10/02/12-great-quotes-from-gandhi-on-his-birthday/.

2 Emily Dickinson, *The Complete Poems of Emily Dickinson*, edited by Thomas H. Johnson (New York: Back Bay Books, 1976), p. 433.

Other Books in the
LIFE Leadership Essentials Series

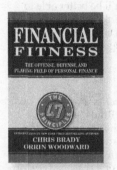

Financial Fitness: The Offense, Defense, and Playing Field of Personal Finance **with Introduction by Chris Brady and Orrin Woodward – $21.95**
If you ever feel that you're too far behind and can't envision a better financial picture, you are so WRONG! You need this book! The *Financial Fitness* book is for everyone at any level of wealth. Just like becoming physically or mentally fit, becoming financially fit requires two things: knowing what to do and taking the necessary action to do it. Learn how to prosper, conserve, and become fiscally fantastic. It's a money thing, and the power to prosper is all yours!

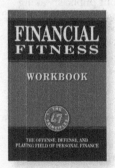

Financial Fitness Workbook – $7.95
Economic affairs don't have to be boring or stressful. Make managing money fun in a few simple steps. Use this workbook to get off to a great start and then continue down the right path to becoming fiscally fabulous! Discover exactly where all of your money actually goes as you make note of all your expenditures. Every page will put you one step closer to financial freedom, so purchase the *Financial Fitness Workbook* today and get budgeting!

Mentoring Matters: Targets, Techniques, and Tools for Becoming a Great Mentor **with Foreword by Orrin Woodward – $19.95**
Get your sticky notes ready for all the info you're about to take in from this book. Do you know what it means to be a *great* mentor? It's a key part of successful leadership, but for most people, the necessary skills and techniques don't come naturally. Educate yourself on all of the key targets, techniques, and tools for becoming a magnificent mentor with this easy-to-apply manual. Your leadership success will be forever increased!

Turn the Page: How to Read Like a Top Leader with Introduction by Chris Brady – $15.95
Leaders are readers. But there are many ways to read, and leaders read differently than most people do. They read to learn what they need to know, do, or feel, regardless of the author's intent or words. They see past the words and read with the specific intent of finding truth and applying it directly in their own lives. Learn how to read like a top leader so you'll be better able to emulate their success. Applying the skills taught in *Turn the Page* will impact your life, career, and leadership abilities in ways you can't even imagine. So turn the page and start reading!

SPLASH!: A Leader's Guide to Effective Public Speaking with Foreword by Chris Brady – $15.95
For many, the fear of giving a speech is worse than the fear of death. But public speaking can be truly enjoyable *and* a powerful tool for making a difference in the lives of others. Whether you are a beginner or a seasoned orator, this book will help you transform your public speaking to a whole new level of leadership influence. Learn the SPLASH formula for great public speaking that will make you the kind of speaker and leader who makes a SPLASH—leaving any audience, big or small, forever changed—every time you speak!

The Serious Power of Fun with Foreword by Chris Brady – $15.95
Life got you down? Feeling like life isn't much fun is a bad place to be. Fun matters. It is serious business and a source of significant leadership power. Without it, few people maintain the levels of inspired motivation and sustained effort that bring great success. So put a smile back on your face. Discover how to make every area of life more enjoyable and turn any situation into the right kind of fun. Learn to cultivate a habit of designed gratification—where life just keeps getting better—and *laugh your way to increased success* with *The Serious Power of Fun!*

Wavemakers: How Small Acts of Courage Can Change the World with Foreword by Chris Brady – $15.95

Every now and then, extraordinary individuals come along who make huge waves and bring about permanent change in the lives of so many that society as a whole is forever altered. Discover from the examples of the various "Wavemakers" showcased in this book how you can make waves of your own and change the world for the better!

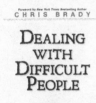

Dealing with Difficult People with Foreword by Chris Brady – $15.95

How many times have you felt like banging your head against the wall trying to figure out how to deal with a routinely difficult person, whether at work or in your personal life? You can't control others, but you can control how you handle them. Learn about the seven main types of difficult people and the Five-Step Peace Process, and equip yourself to understand why people behave the way they do, break the cycle of frustration, and turn your interactions into healthy, productive experiences. "You are going to encounter difficult people. Plan on it. Prepare for it. Become good at it."

Financial Fitness for Teens: 6 Steps from Broke to Abundant with Foreword by Chris Brady – $17.95

It's never too early to learn the principles of financial success. But schools often skip right over this crucial topic. And by the time many adults figure out that they don't know how to properly manage their money, they are often buried in debt and feeling helpless to dig themselves out. *Financial Fitness for Teens* aims to fill in the gap, break the cycle of bad financial habits and misinformation being passed down from generation to generation, and show youth how easy and exciting financial fitness can be. "The money thing" is one of the most important aspects of life to master—and the sooner, the better!

Subscriptions and
Products from
LIFE Leadership

Rascal Radio Subscription – $49.95 per month
Rascal Radio by LIFE Leadership is the world's first online personal development radio hot spot. Rascal Radio is centered on LIFE Leadership's 8 Fs: Faith, Family, Finances, Fitness, Following, Freedom, Friends, and Fun. Subscribers have unlimited access to **hundreds and hundreds** of audio recordings that they can stream endlessly from both the **LIFE Leadership website** and the **LIFE Leadership Smartphone App.** Listen to one of the preset stations or customize your own based on speaker or subject. Of course, you can easily skip tracks or "like" as many as you want. And if you are listening from the website, you can purchase any one of these incredible audios.

Let Rascal Radio provide you with **life-changing information to help you live the life you've always wanted!**

The LIFE Series – $50.00 per month
Here's where LIFE Leadership began—with the now famously followed 8 Fs: Family, Finances, Fitness, Faith, Following, Freedom, Friends, and Fun. This highly recommended series offers a strong foundation on which to build and advance in every area of your daily life. The timeless truths and effective strategies included will reignite passion and inspire you to be your very best. Transform your life for the better and watch how it will create positive change in the lives of those around you. Subscribe today and have the time of your LIFE!

Series includes 4 audios and 1 book monthly and is also available in Spanish and French.

The LLR (Launching a Leadership Revolution) Series – $50.00 per month

There is no such thing as a born leader. Based on the *New York Times* bestseller *Launching a Leadership Revolution* by Chris Brady and Orrin Woodward, this series focuses on teaching leadership skills at every level. The principles and specifics taught in the LLR Series will equip you with all the tools you need for business advancement, community influence, church impact, and even an advantage in your home life. Topics include: leadership, finances, public speaking, goal setting, mentoring, game planning, accountability and tracking of progress, levels of motivation and influence, and leaving a personal legacy. Will you be ready to take the lead when you're called? Subscribe now and learn how to achieve effective confidence skills while growing stronger in your leadership ability.

Series includes 4 audios and 1 leadership book monthly.

The AGO (All Grace Outreach) Series – $25.00 per month

We are all here together to love one another and take care of each other. But sometimes in this hectic world, we lose our way and forget our true purpose. When you subscribe to the AGO Series, you'll gain the valuable support and guidance that every Christian searches for. Nurture your soul, strengthen your faith, and find answers to better understand God's plan for your life, marriage, and children.

Series includes 1 audio and 1 book monthly.

The Edge Series – $10.00 per month

You'll cut in front of the rest of the crowd when you get the *Edge*. Designed for those on the younger side of life, this hard-core, no-frills series promotes self-confidence, drive, and motivation. Get advice, timely information, and true stories of success from interesting talks and fascinating people. Block out the noise around you and learn the principles of self-improvement at an early age. It's a gift that will keep on giving from parent to child. Subscribe today and get a competitive *Edge* on tomorrow.

Series includes 1 audio monthly.

The Freedom Series Subscription – $10.00 per month for 12 months

Freedom must be fought for if it is to be preserved. Every nation and generation needs people who are willing to take a stand for it. Are you one of those brave leaders who'll answer the call? Gain an even greater understanding of the significance and power of freedom, get better informed on issues that affect yours, and find out how you can prevent its decline. This series covers freedom matters that are important to *you*. Make your freedom and liberty a priority and subscribe today.

Subscription includes 1 audio monthly for 12 months.

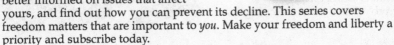

Financial Fitness Subscription – $10.00 per month for 12 months
If you found the *Financial Fitness Pack* life-changing and beneficial to your bank account, then you'll want even more timely information and guidance from the Financial Fitness Subscription. It's designed as a continuing economic education to help people develop financial discipline and overall knowledge of how their money works. Learn how to make financial principles your financial habits. It's a money thing, and it always pays to be cash savvy.

Subscription includes 1 audio monthly for 12 months.

Financial Fitness Pack – $99.99
Once and for all, it's time to free yourself from the worry and heavy burden of debt. Decide today to take an honest look at your finances by learning and applying the simple principles of financial success. The *Financial Fitness Pack* provides you with all the tools needed to get on a path to becoming fiscally fantastic!

Pack includes the Financial Fitness *book, a companion workbook, and 8 audio recordings.*